AF608174

THE CONCEPT OF CLERICAL IMMUNITY

THE CATHOLIC UNIVERSITY OF AMERICA
CANON LAW STUDIES
No. 126

THE CONCEPT OF CLERICAL IMMUNITY

A DISSERTATION IN
PUBLIC ECCLESIASTICAL LAW

Submitted to the Faculty of Canon Law of the Catholic University of America in Partial Fulfillment of the Requirements for the Degree of

DOCTOR OF CANON LAW

BY

REV. JOHN EMMANUEL DOWNS, A.B., J.C.L.
Priest of the Archdiocese of New York

THE CATHOLIC UNIVERSITY OF AMERICA PRESS
WASHINGTON, D. C.
1941

NIHIL OBSTAT:

EDUARDUS G. ROELKER, S.T.D., J.C.D.,
Censor Deputatus.

Washingtonii, D. C., die VIII Maii 1941.

IMPRIMATUR:

✠ FRANCISCUS J. SPELLMAN, D.D.,
Archiepiscopus Neo-Eboracensis.

PRINTED IN THE UNITED STATES OF AMERICA
BY THE WATKINS PRINTING CO., BALTIMORE

TO MY MOTHER
AND TO THE
MEMORY OF MY FATHER

TABLE OF CONTENTS

INTRODUCTION

The concept of clerical immunity exemplifies several of the most controversial problems in the history of the Catholic Church. In its *theoretical aspect* this question reflects the much discussed problem of the precise title of the obligation induced by the secondary principles and remote conclusions of the natural law. In its *practical aspect* it runs through the entire field of the relations between Church and State. In its *social implications* it is an institution that was ground in the very essence of medieval society. But these aspects of the problem, however absorbing they may be to the theologian and the philosopher, the student of political science and the sociologist, are outside the scope of a treatise in public ecclesiastical law.[1] Nevertheless certain conclusions from each of these sciences must be posited before entering into a discussion of the concept of clerical immunity. They are proved elsewhere. Among these are: 1. The indirect superiority in the Church over the State in matters temporal;[2] 2. the distinction between the necessary and immutable and the contingent and variable principles of the natural law, despite the obscurity of the question;[3] and 3. the fact that the *complete exemption* of the clergy in their persons and in their goods is no longer a social necessity.[4] Granted that the changed conditions of modern society no longer require the complete exemption of the clergy from all secular jurisdiction and from any obligation that could be imposed by the State *under the title of jurisdiction,* the judge of this question of fact is not the State, but the Church, inasmuch as

[1] "Scientia iurium et officiorum Ecclesiae tamquam perfectae societatis ex divina eius institutione promanantium."—A. Van Hove, *Prolegomena ad codicem iuris canonici* (Commentarium Lovaniense in codicem iuris canonici, vol. I, tom. I, Mechliniae-Romae: H. Dessain, 1928), p. 34. Hereafter this work will be referred to as *Prolegomena.*

[2] Cf. R. Hull, *Medieval theories of the papacy* (London: Burns, Oates and Washbourne, 1934), Chapp. II-IX.

[3] Van Hove, *Prolegomena,* pp. 42-44.

[4] Cf. L. Sturzo, *Church and State* (New York: Longmans, Green & Co., 1939, pp. 30-47, 326-329, *et alibi passim.*

she is the superior of the two juridically perfect societies. This she can do in either of two ways; either *expressly* by inducing a change in her own law, or *tacitly* by ratifying an already existing civil law or through the admission of a contrary custom derogatory to clerical immunity.

Personal immunity withdraws clerics and religious from secular jurisdiction in matters wherein other citizens would be subject to it; it exempts them from public duties imposed by civil law upon citizens in general. The norm of this exemption of ecclesiastical persons, not in their spiritual offices as ministers of religion, but in their persons and goods considered from a temporal aspect, is its *necessity for the good of the Church.* It is under this aspect that the question is treated in this study. The canonical explanation of the origin, changes in the law and the present discipline of the individual immunities is treated in various commentaries and monographs. In this treatise, however, the discussion is limited to the *concept of the personal immunity of the clergy in its historical and juridical origin.* No attempt is made to discuss individual immunities, except insofar as is necessary in order to demonstrate the attitude of the various schools of thought towards the juridical origin, that is, the precise right or title of the immunity of the clergy. Accordingly, the treatment of the actual discipline regarding clerical immunity, past and present, is only incidental.

Materially, clerical immunity is the sum of exemptions from the secular power which the Church accords to clerics and religious. *Formally,* it is a *jus singulare* which clerics enjoy by right and religious by extension, established by the Church and consisting of their exemption from the jurisdiction of civil courts and from other obligations and duties commonly imposed by the State upon citizens. The juridical perfection of the Church and her consequent independence of the State postulates that clerical immunity in its origin, essence and abolition *cannot be merely of civil law,* although some particular immunities may have originally been concessions by the civil power. In their canonical aspect, the exemptions which comprise clerical immunity are dispositions of ecclesiastical law, made either by the Church herself or received and "canonized" from favors extended by the secular authority. Hence it is perfectly correct to say that clerical immunity is *formally of human law.* But from the viewpoint of public ecclesiastical law this expression is insufficient. The student of public law must pursue his inquiry into the *basis* of clerical exemption; this basis is found ultimately in divine law. But what is the precise right or title of clerical immunity? This is a question that has caused great discussion between canonists and theologians. Its answer is found in the common opinion today. Although formally, proximately and immediately of ecclesiastical law, it is nevertheless *fundamentally, remotely and mediately of divine law;* for in divine law are found the *power* of the Church to exempt her ministers from secular jurisdiction, the *exemplary* causes of immunity and the *final cause of the* exemption. The discussion of the various attitudes towards this question, the refutation of the false view of clerical immunity and the observation of the evolution of a mode of expression which clearly manifests all these elements is the burden of this dissertation.

The *aim* of this study is to outline and observe the principles of the juridical origin of clerical immunity in their development and expression by canonists and theologians. Its *method* is threefold: It consists of the following elements: 1. A brief historical summary of the pertinent factors in the origin and growth of the immunity of the clergy. 2. A presentation and refutation of the false views of this question. 3. An examination of the thought actually intended and expressed by canonists and theologians in their attitude towards its juridical origin.

In the *historical synopsis* special emphasis is directed towards the chief sources from which the various views of clerical immunity were derived—the papal documents and decrees of the councils. A proper understanding of these is the best refutation of the adversaries of the Church. In the *Juridical inquiry,* which is devoted to an analysis of the precise right or title by which clerical immunity can exist, the various forms of approach to the problem are presented and evaluated. These are commonly grouped into four main schools of thought; namely, 1. the opinion of the Protestants, regalists and present-day liberals *that clerical immunity is based purely upon civil law;* 2. the opinion of Suarez and many of the older canonists *that this prerogative of the clergy is formally of divine law;* 3. the view of the theologians that *this class of exemption is not of divine, but is of ecclesiastical law;* and finally, 4. the true opinion, which has become the common view, *that the immunities of the clergy are formally of human law, ecclesiastical and civil; but that there is, nevertheless a true basis for them in divine law.*

The first of these opinions must be rejected; it is contrary to the doctrine that the Church is a juridically perfect society. The true concept of clerical immunity is found in the *via media* between what had formerly been referred to as "the view of the canonists" and "the view of the theologians." The object of this study is to present and evaluate these views, and to trace the rise and growth of the doctrine now common among ecclesiastical writers.

An evaluation of the opinions of canonists and theologians indicates that "one school of thought affirmed what the other school did not deny." Yet, although both sides maintained the solid probability of the other's view, they arrived at contrary conclusions. They differed in their approach to the problem and in their understanding of the concept; but as a more clear and more precise terminology was evolved, two apparently divergent views became fused into what is practically the universal opinion among Catholics today. No hint can be gleaned from any author of modern times regarding the "Gordion knot" that the problem of clerical immunity once presented. The precise basis of the exemption of the clergy is now firmly established, as all modern Catholic authors admit. The fascinating canonical history and public law inquiry regarding the juridical concept of their immunity from secular jurisdiction and from certain common civil obligations are discussed in the pages that follow.

The writer avails himself of this opportunity to express his gratitude to Their Excellencies, the Most Reverend Francis J. Spellman, D.D., Archbishop of New York, the Most Reverend Stephen J. Donaghue, D.D., and the Most Reverend J. Francis A. McIntyre, D.D. for the opportunity afforded him for graduate study. He acknowledges with sincere appreciation the helpful direction in the preparation of this study accorded by the Reverend members of the Faculty of the School of Canon Law of the Catholic University.

To these and to other friends unnamed, sincere thanks are expressed. Their kindness and helpfulness has been the source of many happy memories during the preparation of this dissertation.

PART I

PRENOTES AND HISTORICAL SYNOPSIS

CHAPTER I

PRENOTES

CLERICAL IMMUNITY, or the exemption of ecclesiastical persons from the jurisdiction of secular tribunals and from certain obligations which civil law imposes upon citizens,[1] is, as Boudinhon observes, "a chapter in the more extensive history of the relations of Church and State."[2] Consequently it is related in one way or another to the various problems which exist by reason of this relationship.

I. The concept of clerical exemption from civil jurisdiction formerly included the exemption of clerics from civil laws.[3] Although all Catholic writers have agreed that although members of the clergy are citizens, not all have been willing to admit that they were obliged to observe civil laws simply in that and no other capacity. The common and true doctrine today is that they are bound by the *efficacy of civil laws themselves* in all matters which do not run counter to the prescriptions of canon law, although they are exempt from secular jurisdiction in the strict sense of the judicial and coercive power of secular magistrates,[4]

[1] F. Schmalzgrueber, *Ius ecclesiasticum universum* ([ ] ed., 5 vols. in 12, Romae, 1843-1845), lib. II, tit. II, n. 73, and lib. III, tit. XLIX, n. 1; F. Cavagnis, *Institutiones iuris publici ecclesiastici* (3. ed., 3 vols., Romae, 1883), II, 176; F. X. Wernz, *Ius decretatium* (2. ed., 6 toms., Romae, 1906-1913), II, n. 168, and III, nn. 445-449; F. Cappello, *Summa iuris publici ecclesiastici* (2. ed., Romae: apud aedes Universitatis Gregorianae, 1928), pp. 453-454; M. Conte a Coronata, *Ius publicum ecclesiasticum* (2. ed., Taurini: Marietti, 1934), p. 194; A. Ottaviani, *Institutiones iuris publici ecclesiastici* (2. ed., 2 vols., Romae: Typis Polyglottis Vaticanis, 1935-1936), I, 390.

[2] "Immunity"—*Catholic encyclopedia* (15 vols. and 2 supplements, New York, 1907-1922), VII, 690.

[3] C. 10, X. *de constitutionibus,* I, II.

[4] Wernz, *Ius decretalium,* I, n. 108; Cavagnis, *Institutiones iuris publici ecclesiastici,* II, n. 154; P. De Angelis, *Praelectiones iuris canonici* ([ ] ed., Romae, 1908), lib. I, pars I, n. 13; Cappello, *Summa iuris publici ecclesiastici,* pp. 164-165. Ottaviani, *Institutiones iuris publici ecclesiastici,* I, 392-393.

unless legitimate provision to the contrary has been made for particular places.[5]

II. Clerical immunity is a part of the general concept of ecclesiastical immunity; the former is exemption from civil jurisdiction *ratione personae,* the latter is exemption *ratione materiae* and includes the idea of local and real immunity, although the latter are properly applications of the native right of the Church to administer her own temporal affairs.[6]

III. A distinction must be made between the *historical origin* and the *juridical origin* of clerical immunity. The former comprises the actual historical facts which indicate that the clergy acquired exemption from civil jurisdiction; the latter is the precise right or title whereby the clergy can be said to enjoy this exemption by *divine* as well as by *human law.*

Clerical immunity is a corollary and an exemplification of the broader concept of the liberty and independence of the Church from secular interference; the latter is not properly an immunity, but a native right which flows from the juridical perfection of the Church.[7] As Coronata observes, much confusion on this point has arisen due to the failure of many writers to observe this distinction.[8] Nevertheless it must be pointed out that any offense against clerical immunity is an offense against the liberty of the Church and a violation of the right of ecclesiastical jurisdiction. This must be kept in mind in order to appreciate the vigorous protests of the Holy See against the usurpation of ecclesiastical jurisdiction and the violation of immunity.

IV. The concept of clerical immunity must be differentiated from the cognate question of the absolute exemption of the Roman Pontiff by divine law from all human power. Authors in

[5] Canon 120, § 1.

[6] A. Reiffenstuel, *Ius canonicum universum* (5 vols. in 7, Monachii, 1702), lib. III, tit. XLIX, n. 3.

[7] Canon 1553, § 1, 3°, which declares the proper and exclusive right of the Church to judge all cases, whether they be contentious or criminal, of those who enjoy the privilege of the forum, is an example of this *native right;* the persons mentioned in the canon enjoy the *immunity.*

[8] *Ius publicum ecclesiasticum,* p. 194 and note 1.

public ecclesiastical law consistently observe this distinction, and separate their discussion of the common immunities of clerics from that of the personal immunity of the Holy Father.[9] The latter question implies a right that the Vicar of Christ enjoys *immediately by divine law;* the former is the point under discussion in this thesis.[10]

The concept of ecclesiastical immunity as illustrated in the various sources of canon law from the time of Constantine the Great (306-337) to the present day is the exemption of sacred persons, places and things from civil jurisdiction and from certain common obligations of citizens that are incompatible, either in whole or in part, with their sacred status; and implies the right of the Church to effect these exemptions, notwithstanding the existence of a valid statute of the civil law to the contrary. This broad concept of exemption may rest upon a twofold basis: it may be either *formally of divine law* in the case of strictly spiritual matters or of native rights of the Church as the supreme perfect society in temporal matters; or it may be *formally of ecclesiastical law* and even of civil law, in the case of immunity in the strict sense of the term. This broad concept has been the object of several explicit declarations of the Church that ecclesiastical and clerical immunity exists not only by reason of human law, but by divine law as well.[11]

[9] Thus Cavagnis, *Institutiones,* II, 197-199; Cappello, *Summa,* 478-481; Coronata, *Ius publicum ecclesiasticum,* pp. 219-222.

[10] Accordingly there is a different juridical basis for the penalties mentioned in canon 2343, § 1, than there is for those mentioned in the other sections of this canon.

[11] The more famous of these include the statement of Pope Boniface VIII (1294-1303): "Cum igitur ecclesiae, ecclesiasticaque personae ac res ipsarum non solum iure humano, quin immo et divino a saecularium personarum exactionibus sint immunes."—c. 4, *de censibus, exactionibus et procurationibus,* III, 20, in VI°; that of Pope Leo X (1513-1521), Ap. Const. *"Supernae dispositionis,"* 5 maii 1514: "Et cum a iure tam divino quam humano laicis potestas nulla in Ecclesasticas personas attributa sit"—*Codicis iuris canonici fontes cura Emi. Card. Gasparri editi* (9 vols., Romae [later, Civitate Vaticana]: Typis Polyglottis Vaticanis, 1923-1939, Vols. VII-IX ed. *cura et studio Emi. Justiniani Card.*

It is natural that in these documents emphasis is placed *primarily* upon the divine right of ecclesiastical jurisdiction in virtue of which the Church can decree the exemption of her ministers—even in their civil capacities—from State laws that validly bind other citizens, and *secondarily* upon the effect of this right, or the notion of clerical immunity as such. An analysis of the interpretations of these statements by canonists and theologians, however, reveals that it is often quite difficult to separate those elements of the broader concept of immunity which are *preceptively* of divine law from those which are *strongly in accord* with divine law or natural equity but not quite the objects of a strict precept in justice. It is to this latter group that the clerical immunities belong. Those in the past who were inclined to give a strictly literal interpretation to these texts in their application of them to the entire concept of immunity fell into this pitfall. Although they based their position upon the exact words of the text, they did not sufficiently explain (in the opinion of those who held the contrary view) that the texts themselves do not determine the sense in which the words *divine law* were used. Coronata points this out in his criticism of those who held this view.[12]

The solemn declarations of the Supreme Pontiffs and the canons of innumerable councils have always placed emphasis upon the proper and exclusive right of the Church to judge all matters *de fide et sacerdotibus;* it is stated explicitly again in the Code.[13] Some of these declarations have included the proposition that

Serédi), n. 65, § 40 (Hereafter this collection will be referred to as *Fontes*); and that of the Council of Trent (1545-1563): "Ecclesiae et personarum ecclesiasticarum immunitatem Dei ordinatione et canonicis sanctionibus constitutam"—Sess. XX, cap. 20, *de ref.*—*Canones et decreta sacrosancti concilii oecumenici Tridentini* ([ ] ed., Romae, 1845), pp. 219-220. Cf. also Pius IX, litt. ap. *"Multiplices inter,"* 10 iun. 1851—*Fontes,* n. 510; Propositions 30, 31, 32, *Syllabus errorum Pii IX*—H. Denzinger, G. Bannwart, J. Umberg, *Enchiridion symbolorum definitionum et declarationum de rebus fidei et morum* (21-23 ed., Friburgi Brisgoviae: Herder & Co., 1937), nn. 1730, 1731, 1732. Hereafter this collection will be referred to as *Enchiridion Symbolorum.*

[12] Ius publicum ecclesiasticum, p. 208.

[13] Canon 1553.

lay persons have no power over the persons or goods of ecclesiastics.[14] All Catholic writers, especially since the Council of Trent (1545-1563), have observed the distinction between the exemption of the clergy in regard to strictly sacred matters on the one hand, and in their civil and criminal processes on the other. In view of this distinction every canonical writer since Schmalzgrueber (†1735) [15] has accepted the terminology, which he adopted from Pirhing († 1679),[16] that immunities in the strict sense are *originaliter et initiative* of divine law, but *proxime et formaliter* of ecclesiastical law. However, accidental variations of this expression can be noted among present day authors. Cappello,[17] Coronata [18] and Ottaviani [19] concur that it is now commonly agreed that the most tenable interpretation of the statements of the *magisterium* of the Church regarding the juridical origin of clerical immunity is that it arises *fundamentally, basically, mediately and remotely from divine law, but that formally, immediately and proximately it is of ecclesiastical law,* either constituted by the Church herself on her own authority or ratified and sanctioned by her from civil laws and customs that grew up in favor of the immunity of the clergy.

[14] Cf. *supra*, p. 3 and note 11.

[15] *Ius canonicum universum*, lib. II, tit. II, n. 98.

[16] Pirhing himself rejected the view—E. Pirhing, *Ius canonicum in V libros decretalium distributum* ([ ] ed., Dillingae, 1774), lib. II, tit. II, sect. III, n. 110.

[17] "Hodie communis est eaque vera dicenda."—*Summa*, p. 458.

[18] Hanc opinionem admittunt plures antiquiores et fere omnes ex modernis auctoribus; unde vere communior est dicenda."—*Ius publicum ecclesiasticum*, p. 209.

[19] *Institutiones*, I, 406.

Chapter II

CLERICAL IMMUNITY FROM THE FOURTH TO THE TWELFTH CENTURY

The period from the Decree of Milan (312) to the Constitution of the Emperor Frederick II on the occasion of his coronation (1220) represents the time *prior to the full guarantee* of total exemption of clerics and their goods in civil law. During this period clerical immunity flourished in a more or less restricted degree. The popes struggled to maintain the exclusive competence of the Church in all cases *de fide et sacerdotibus,* and councils protected the exemption of the clergy insofar as local conditions would permit. Especially during the eleventh century reform movement of Pope Gregory VII (1073-1085) the Holy See firmly upheld the principle that lay persons may exercise no jurisdiction over clerics. Although the *principle* of the independence of the Church was strongly urged, the many protests of popes and councils against usurpations of ecclesiastical jurisdiction during these centuries indicate that the concept of complete clerical exemption was not yet realized *in fact.* Although strongly urged in ecclesiastical law, clerical immunity in the sense of a complete exemption of the clergy from civil jurisdiction was not yet fully respected in civil law.

Article 1. Clerical Immunity in the Roman Empire

In the Roman Empire, after the famous Decree of Milan, the clergy enjoyed many rights or privileges of exemption from the necessity of observing *munera* [1] or legal obligations that were binding upon citizens in general. Constantine accorded to the churches and clergy an unrestricted and unqualified exemption from all public obligations.[2] The Roman emperors realized that by reason of their sacred character the clergy should be exempt

[1] "Munus proprie est quod necessario obimus lege more imperiove eius qui iubendi habet potestatem."—Marcianus in D. (50, 16) 214.

[2] C. Th. (11, 1) 1.

from public duties incompatible with their exalted vocation. In view of the expense they bore in the care of the poor, the clergy were free from the obligation to pay certain taxes.[3] The general exemptions given by Constantine (306-307) were qualified by his successors, who enlarged or restricted existing immunities and added others as well.[4] Constantius, the successor of Constantine (337-361), revoked nearly all clearical immunities;[5] before his death, however, he restored the exemption from personal and extraordinary obligations.[6] These exemptions were sanctioned by Valentinian I (364-375), extended by Gratianus (375-395),[7] although these emperors enacted no essentially new legislation. In general they confirmed the freedom of the clergy from military and curial srvice, from the strict obligation of undertaking *tutela* and *cura,* from all menial tasks, etc. Valentinian III (425-455) restricted the list of menial tasks and declared that certain public obligations had to be undertaken by all citizens "without exemption of reverence or dignity." [8] At times these privileges were revoked by an emperor or extended to clerics who were members of heretical sects. In this case they were restored or properly aligned by his successor.[9]

The legislation of the Code of Justinian repeated the provisions of the earlier emperors in the matter of clerical immunity with only slight modifications. The churches and clergy were declared free from extraordinary or mental obligations, from new tasks,

[3] C. Th. (16, 2) 2.

[4] O. Grashof, "Die Gesetze der römischen Kaiser über die Immunitäten des Klerus"—*Archiv für katholisches Kirchenrecht* (Innsbruck, 1857-1861; Mainz, 1862—), XXXVII (1877), 257-258. Hereafter this periodical will be referred to as *AKKR.*

[5] C. Th. (16, 2) 15.

[6] C. Th. (16, 2) 26. The wording of this edict is significant; it is the keynote of the legislation of those emperors who were favorable to the Church: *"Gaudere enim et gloriari ex fide semper volumus, scientes magis religionibus quam officiis et labore corporis vel sudore nostram rempublicam contineri."*

[7] C. Th. (16, 2) 24 & 26.

[8] N. Th. 21.

[9] C. Th. (16, 2) 38 & 47.

from liability for the quartering of troops, and from common personal civic duties.[10]

With regard to privileged jurisdiction for the clergy the imperial legislation varied. In general the emperors verified the competence of the Church in spiritual matters and points of ecclesiastical discipline.[11] Rufinus (*c.* 345-410) records that at the Council of Nice (325) Constantine declined to adjudicate the case submitted to him by the bishops on the ground of his own incompetence over the sacred persons of the fathers.[12] The words which Rufinus attributed to Constantine were later to become an object of much dispute in the controversy over the juridical origin of clerical immunity.

Constantius removed charges against bishops from the competence of the secular courts. These, he. decreed, could be tried only by their fellow bishops.[13] Dr. Boyd observes that in this constitution can be found the origin and precedent for the examination of criminal charges against bishops by the ecclesiastical authorities prior to any action in the secular courts.[14] Gratianus (375-383) decreed that only contentious cases and minor offences were to be tried before the synods, while their criminal trials were to take place only before the civil magistrates.[15] The III

[10] C. (1, 2) 3; (1, 3) 1-2; (1, 3) 6.

[11] P. de Francisci, *Per la storia dell' episcopalis audientiá* (Roma: Athenaeum, 1915), p. 7.

[12] *Historia ecclesiastica,* lib. X, cap. 2: "Deus vos constituit sacerdotes . . . et ideo nos a vobis recte iudicamur; *vos autem non potestis ab hominibus* iudicari. Propter quod Dei solius inter vos expectate iudicium: et *vestra iurgia quaecumque sunt,* ad illud divinum reserventur examen. Vos autem nobis a Deo dati estis Dii: et convenies non est ut homo iudicet deos; sed ille solus de quo scriptum est: Deus stetit in synogoga deorum, in medio autem deos discernit."—J. P. Migne, *Patrologiae cursus completus, Series Latina* (221 vols., Parisiis, 1844-1855), XXI, 468. Hereafter this collection will be referred to as *MPL.*

[13] C. Th. (16, 2) 12.

[14] W. Boyd, *The ecclesiastical edicts of the Theodosian Code* (*Studies in History, Economics and Public Law, edited by the Faculty of Political Science of Columbia University,* vol. XXIV, N. 2, New York: The Columbia University Press, 1905), p. 92.

[15] C. Th. (16, 2) 23.

Council of Carthage (397) however, decreed that clerics be judged by ecclesiastics and not by laymen.[16] The Emperor Honorius (395-423) abrogated the restriction of Gratianus, and explicitly decreed that all orders of the clergy were to be accused only in the tribunal of the bishops.[17] Valentinian III (425-455) in the year following the Council of Chalcedon (451) decreed that a cleric could be convened in a civil court in either a contentious or a criminal case; that bishops were not exempt from the jurisdiction of civil courts, although in criminal cases they could plead through a procurator; that disputes between members of the clergy could be settled in the bishop's court only if both parties so agreed; and that a cleric acting as petitioner against a layman had to go before the civil court unless the defendnt agreed to an ecclesiastical hearing.[18] Notwithstanding this enactment, at least two councils in Gaul reiterated the ecclesiastical prohibition of the Council of Chalcedon [19] against clerics having recourse to secular courts without the consent of their bishop. These were the Councils of Angers (c. 453-455) [20] and of Vannes (465).[21] The law of Valentinian was repealed by Majorianus (457-461).[22]

Justinian decreed that, although in ecclesiastical matters the court of the bishop was the necessary forum, contentious cases of the clergy either among themselves or with layfolk could be brought before the episcopal tribunal only if the parties consented.[23] Later it was necessary for him to reprobate the abuse of filing suit against monks and nuns in civil courts. He defi-

[16] C. 8: "Ut clerici ecclesiastici ordinis si culpam incurrerint, apud ecclesiasticos iudicentur, non apud saeculares."—J. Harduin, *Acta conciliorum et epistolae decretales ac constitutiones summorum pontificum* (12 vols., Parisiis, 1715), I, 962. Hereafter this collection will be referred to as *Acta Conciliorum*.

[17] C. Th. 16, 2) 41.

[18] N. Val. (3, 34) pr.

[19] C. 9.—Harduin, *Acta Conciliorum*, II, 606.

[20] C. 1.—Harduin· *Acta Conciliorum*, II, 778.

[21] C. 2.—Harduin, *Acta Conciliorum*, II, 797.

[22] O. Grashof, "Die Annerkennung des privilegirten Gerichsstands des Klerus durch die römischen Kaiser"—*AKKR*, XXXVIII (1877), 17.

[23] C. (1, 4) 7.

nitely established that the examination of their cases be the exclusive concern of the bishops.[24] In criminal actions against the clergy he allowed only certain *cautiones* for the protection of the dignity of the clerical state, but the cases themselves he definitely committed to the civil judges,[25] although he provided that no *bishop* could be brought unwillingly before a secular or military court without a mandate from the emperor.[26]

It will be noted that Roman law made some provision for the settlement of contentious cases before the episcopal court; certainly the clergy could, and were required by the law of the councils to submit their cases which arose from differences among themselves to the bishops for adjudication. The precise nature of the episcopal court is not under discussion here. Whether it was a court empowered by Constantine with full magisterial powers in the eyes of Roman law, or a court of arbitration, is a very interesting question. Many authors.[27] whose opinion is shared by canonists of note,[28] hold that it was a tribunal in the strict sense of the term. Their conclusion depends upon the authenticity of two constitutions of Constantine,[29] which is contested by several noted writers.[30] Francisci adduces several strong intrinsic and extrinsic arguments against the authenticity of these constitutions, and shows that the position of bishops as arbiters and not as judges in contentious cases was eminently in keeping with the genius of Roman law.[31]

If, on the other hand, the opinion commonly accepted among

[24] N. 79.

[25] C. (1, 4) 29; N. (123, 23); cf. N. 83.

[26] N. (123, 8).

[27] E.g., Haenel, Bethmann-Hollweck, Witte, Loening, Cuq, Martroye, cited by Francisci, *Per la storia dell' episcopalis audientiá,* p. 11.

[28] E.g., Cappello, *Summa,* p. 460; Coronata, *Ius publicum ecclesiasticum,* p. 199; Ottaviani, *Institutiones,* I, 320-321.

[29] C. Th. (1, 27) I (Const. Sirmond. XVII); and Const. Sirmond. I—Mommsen, *Corpus iuris civilis* (5 [15] ed., 3 vols., Berolini), *Prolegomena,* CCCLXXX.

[30] Gothofredus, Savigny, Haubold, Hugo, Blum, Eichhorn, Krüger are cited by Francisci, *Per la storia dell' episcopalis audientiá,* p. 11.

[31] *Op. cit.,* pp. 12-31.

canonists is true, it must be concluded with Dr. Boyd that the recognition of the episcopal court as a source of secular justice is unique in the history of Roman jurisprudence. Boyd argues that inasmuch as the first legislation upon the subject is lost, no definite interpretation of the bishops' position is possible. Moreover, if this opinion be true, it is not improbable that the bishops regarded the privilege given them by Constantine as a step towards the exemption of the clergy from the civil courts.[32] But, notwithstanding the testimony of Sozomen († c. 450) regarding Constantine's legislation in this matter,[33] the unique character of this privilege, together with the absence of any reference to it either by the councils or the other emperors, are the very reasons why Francisci insists in his denial of its authenticity.[34]

Notwithstanding the prescriptions of Roman law, however, the councils of Carthage [35] and Mileve (416) [36] and the II Council of Arles (442) [37] laid down definite norms for the trials of clerics, both contentious and criminal, and decreed that no secular judge could presume to adjudicate the case of a cleric without the knowledge and consent of his bishop, and forbade clerics to desert the episcopal tribunal and have recourse to the secular courts. These provisions were incorporated into the enactments of the IV Ecumenical Council, that of Chalcedon (451).[38]

In the minds of the Fathers as well as in the decrees of the early councils, the concept *Ecclesia judicat de fide et sacerdotibus* was not weakened by a distinction between strictly spiritual cases of clerics and their contentious and criminal trials.

[32] *The ecclesiastical edicts of the Theodosian Code,* p. 92.

[33] *Historia ecclesiastica,* lib. I, cap. IX—J. P. Migne, *Patrologiae cursus completus, series graeca* (161 vols., Parisiis: 1857-1866), LVII, 884. Hereafter this collection will be referred to as *MPG.*

[34] *Per la storia dell' episcopalis audientiá,* p. 25.

[35] III Carthage (397), c. 9—Harduin, *Acta Conciliorum,* I, 962; VIII Carthage (403), c. 22; XI Carthage (407), c. 114—Harduin, *Acta Conciliorum,* I, 923.

[36] C. 19—Harduin, *Acta Conciliorum,* I, 1220.

[37] C. 31—Harduin, *Acta Conciliorum,* II, 775.

[38] C. 9—Harduin, *Acta Conciliorum,* II, 606.

This is evident from a letter of St. Hilary († 366) to the emperor Constantine II (337-340), in which Hilary complained that certain provincial officials had been guilty of presumption and usurpation because they took it for granted that they could try the cases of clerics.[39] St. Ambrose († 397) bitterly castigated the conduct of Palladius at the Council of Aquilea (381), who, upon being accused of Arianism, refused to reply to the bishops at the Council, but appealed to the imperial court. The words of St. Ambrose give an indication of the strong feeling that prevailed in the early Church regarding the abuse of clerics who would presume to violate the principle: *Ecclesia iudicat de fide et sacerdotibus,* when he declared: *"Erubescimus ut videatur, qui sacerdotium sibi vindicat, a laicis esse damnatus."* [40]

Article 2. Clerical Immunity in New Christian Nations

Under the Merovingian kings and the Carolingian emperors further immunities were accorded the clergy in view of their sacred character and in virtue of their civil position as well.[41] These privileges included the exemption of certain ecclesiastical lands and other goods from royal taxes, the immunity of clerics and their servants from certain public obligations. and eventually the removal of limitations attached to the privilege of the forum. At first these privileges were granted by the pope or by the king, always at the request of individual bishops and abbots. They became quite common and exerted much influence in the establishment of general customs, and to a certain extent were the basis for the complete immunity from secular jurisdiction which the Church vindicated for the clergy.[42]

In the Visigothic kingdom, the III Council of Toledo (589),

[39] *MPL* X, 557.

[40] *MPL* XVI, 952.

[41] J. Hergenröther, *Catholic Church and Christian State* (2 vols. in 1, London, 1876), Essay VI, part I, nn. 8-9.

[42] Many examples of these rescripts are contained in the *Codex diplomaticus* of Charlemagne (*MPL* XCVII, 913-1087) and in J. von Pflugh-Hartung, *Acta pontificum romanorum inedita* (3 vols., Tübingen, 1881-1886).

by the command and consent of the king, decreed for clerics the immunity from public taxes,[43] threatened excommunication upon any judge or public official who would compel the clergy to undergo public obligations or servile duties, and requested that the king take action against this abuse.[44] Similar exemption was accorded to all freeborn clergymen by the IV Council of Toledo (633) at the command of the king.[45] The influence of royal authority in these matters is an indication that the clergy could as yet enjoy only such exemptions as were decreed by the command of the king.

Under the Merovingian kings immunities were granted by royal decrees and incorporated into the conciliar legislation.[46] The status of the privileged forum of the clergy during this time is evident from the provisions of many local provincial councils. The Church was not yet able to enforce her exclusive jurisdiction over all cases of ecclesiastics, criminal as well as civil. In general the following prescriptions obtained: clerics were strictly forbidden to bring their fellow clerics before a secular judge; bishops were to be tried only before the synods; complaints against the clergy should be tried by a civil judge only with the knowledge and consent of the bishop; criminal trials of clerics were conducted by secular judges, but canonical and not civil sanctions were applied to the guilty party.[47] That a practically uniform discipline existed throughout Gaul in this matter is attested by the similar decrees of the councils of Agde (506),[48] Epaon (517),[49] III Orleans (538),[50] IV Orleans (541),[51] Auxerre

[43] C. 8—H. Bruns, *Canones apostolorum et conciliorum saeculorum IV, V, VI, VII* (2 vols., Berolini, 1839), I, 214. Hereafter this collection will be referred to as *Canones*.

[44] C. 21—Bruns, *Canones*, I, 218.

[45] C. 47—Bruns, *Canones*, I, 235.

[46] E.g., I Orleans (511), c. 5—Bruns, *Canones*, II, 162; III Orleans (538), c. 17—Bruns, Canones, II, 197.

[47] I Conc. Macon (581), c. 7—Bruns, *Canones*, II, 242.

[48] Cc. 8 & 32—Bruns, *Canones*, II, 147 & 152.

[49] C. 11—Bruns, *Canones*, II, 168.

[50] C. 32—Bruns, *Canones*, II, 201.

[51] C. 20—Bruns, *Canones*, II, 206.

(c. 578-585),[52] I Macon (581),[53] II Macon (585)[54] and V Paris (615).[55] The enactments of these synods indicate that a high degree of immunity was enjoyed by all clerics in the sixth and seventh centuries.

Charlemagne definitely established that the clergy were not subject to any personal taxes aside from their ecclesiastical obligations in regard to certain Church property, but were bound to render "due service" in regard to other properties.[56] The Collection of Benedict the Deacon makes note of a "general supplication of all the people to the prince" requesting that priests be excused from personal military service, and the response of the emperor to this request.[57] The capitularies of Charlemagne contain reenactments of the earlier synods in reference to the privileged forum of the clergy.[58] Three councils celebrated during this time are of special note insofar as they asserted the principle that lay persons are prohibited from impeding the exercise of ecclesiastical jurisdiction — the underlying principle of clerical immunity.[59] Although all restrictions had been removed from one particular immunity—the proper forum of the clergy—during the reign of Charlemagne, it would not be quite correct to say that clerical immunity had completely emerged even by this time. The *sacerdotium* was not yet completely free of domination by the *imperium*. After the death of Charlemagne the relationship

[52] C. 35—Bruns, *Canones,* II, 240.

[53] Cc. 7-8—Bruns, *Canones,* II, 243.

[54] Cc. 9-10—Bruns, *Canones,* II, 252.

[55] C. 4—Bruns, *Canones,* II, 256.

[56] *Capitulare ab Ansegiso collecto,* n .85—*MPL,* XCVII, 515.

[57] *Benedicti diaconi capitularium collectio,* II, n. 570—*MPL* XCVII, 788.

[58] E.g., *Capitulare ecclesiasticum* (789), nn. 28 & 38—*Capitularia regum francorum, Monumenta Germaniae historica, Legum sectio* I (5 toms., edd. A. Boretius et V. Krause, Hannoverae, 1897) I, nn. 58 & 80. Hereafter this collection will be referred to as *MGH.*

[59] VI Council of Arles (813), c. 4—Harduin, *Acta Conciliorum,* IV, 1004; Council of Mayence (813), c. 8—Harduin, *Acta Conciliorum,* IV, 1010; III Council of Tours (813), c. 33—Harduin, *Acta Conciliorum,* IV, 1027.

between Church and State grew less favorable, and the oppression of the clergy by the secular power was deplored by councils which were unable to take definite action, however, until the reform movement initiated by Pope Gregory VII (1073-1085).

Article 3. The Action of the Holy See From the Fourth to the Eleventh Century

As early as the year 324, Pope St. Sylvester I (314-335) forbade clerics for any cause to enter the civil curia under most severe penalties.[60]

The letters of Popes Innocent I (404-417), Leo I (440-481), Gelasius I (492-496), Pelagius I (556-561) and Gregory I (590-604) clearly indicate the firm stand of the Holy See in upholding the tradition that all cases which involve ecclesiastical persons be judged in the court of the bishops, or—if in a secular court—with at least the knowledge and consent of the bishop. Innocent I, in a letter to Victricius, Bishop of Rouen, insisted that all cases between clerics be terminated by the bishops of the province.[61] Leo the Great, in a letter to the emperors Valentinian III and Theodosius II, indicated the intimate connection between strictly spiritual matters and the question of jurisdiction over the clergy, and clearly enunciated the traditional doctrine of the exclusive competence of the Church over all such cases when he wrote: *"Beatissimus Romanae civitatis episcopus . . . locum habet ac facultatem de fide et sacerdotibus judicare."* [62] Two letters are ascribed to Gelasius. One was addressed to a certain Count Ezechias and stated that a cleric was not to be heard by a lay judge; the other was sent to two bishops, Crispin and Sabina, and decreed that a cleric was to be called only before the episcopal tribunal.[63] Although Berardi († 1768) states that neither of these decretals is authentic,[64]

[60] Synod of Rome (324), c. 16—Harduin, *Acta Conciliorum,* I, 293.
[61] Epist. II (a. 404), cap. III—*MPL* XX, 472.
[62] Epist. LIII (a. 450)—*MPL* LIV, 657.
[63] Cc. 12 & 13, C. XI, q. 1.
[64] C. Berardi, *Gratiani canones genuini ab apocryphis discreti* (4 toms., Venetiis, 1777), II, 337-339.

both are recorded in the collections of Migne[65] and Thiel († 1908).[66] In his letter to the oriental bishops regarding the excommunication of Accacius, who had appealed to the emperor and whose plea the latter had accepted, Gelasius observed that this was contrary to all ecclesiastical practice and could not be excused merely on the ground that the emperor professed the Catholic faith, and clearly stated that by the ordinance of God, cases involving the person of a priest were in no way within the competence of the emperor, but pertained exclusively to the Church.[67] Gelasius, moreover, congratulated Theodoric (493-526), king of the Ostrogoths, for his action in referring to the pope the examination of two refractory clerics.[68] The privileged forum was definitely recognized by Athalric (526-534) in a decree to the clergy of Rome, as recorded by Cassiodorus († 570).[69]

The pontificate of Gregory the Great (590-604) is noteworthy in regard to the history of clerical immunity inasmuch as several letters written by him portray the firm stand taken by the Holy See against the usurpation of ecclesiastical jurisdiction by the lay power. In letters to Vitalis, the Defender of Sardinia,[70] and to Bishop Januarius of Sardinia,[71] Gregory demanded that the authority of the bishop be upheld lest ecclesiastical discipline collapse, and in three letters to John the Defender, whom he had delegated to try a certain case in Spain, laid down the norms to be followed in all cases which involved the clergy. In every

[65] *MPL* LIX, 151.

[66] A. Thiel, *Epistolae romanorum pontificum genuinae a S. Hilario usque ad Pelagium II* (2 toms., Brunsbergae, 1868), I, n. 293.

[67] Epist. XV (a. 495), c. 10—Thiel, *Epistolae*, n. 295.

[68] *Bullarium diplomatum et privilegiorum sanctorum romanorum Taurinensis editio* (ed. a Francisco Gaudé, 24 vols. & appendix, Augustae Taurinorum, 1857-1872), *appendix*, p. 306. References to the *Bullarium Romanum* throughout this study point to the *Bullarium Romanum Taurinense*.

[69] *Variarum liber VIII*, epist. 24—*MPL* LXIX, 757.

[70] IX, 203—*Gregorii I Papae registrum epistolarum* (edd. P. Ewald et M. Hartmann, t. I in 2 partes), *Epistolarum sectio II*, I, n. 190, in *MGH*.

[71] IX, 204—*Epistolarum sectio II*, I, n. 191, in *MGH*.

case the trial was to be ecclesiastical.[72] In a letter to Romanus, the Defender of Sicily, Gregory protested against the abuse whereby trials had been conducted against clerics without the knowledge and consent of their bishops, and demanded the cessation of these practices.[73] It is to be observed that these letters of Pope Gregory I were concerned directly with violations of the right of the Church to exercise exclusive jurisdiction over the clergy. This is the *basis* of clerical immunity, but it is not formally immunity itself. Inasmuch as any offense against clerical immunity is at the same time a usurpation of ecclesiastical jurisdiction, it is not difficult to understand the grave concern of the pope in this matter.

Another famous declaration regarding the exclusive and native competence of the Church to adjudicate all members of the clergy was made in the ninth century, by Pope Nicholas I (858-867) in a letter to the Emperor Michael III (842-867). The pope once again affirmed the attitude of the Holy See that the civil power is incompetent in all matters *defide et sacerdotibus* and indicated that it is preposterous for those whose competence is limited to human affairs to presume to judge those who have the care of spiritual matters.[74] In this letter, as in those of Popes Gregory, Pelagius, Leo and Gelasius, no distinction was made between strictly civil and religious matters. In civil and criminal cases, unless proper delegation had been given by the Church, the incompetence of civil magistrates, and even of the emperor himself, was openly declared by the Roman Pontiffs.

In the eleventh century, one effect of the reform movement of Pope Gregory VII was to bring about a clearer statement than had existed before regarding the incompetence of lay authorities over the clergy. This had its effect in regard to the concept of

[72] XIII, 47, 49, 50—*Epistolarum sectio* II, nn. 410, 414, 415.

[73] XI, 24—*Epistolarum sectio II,* II, n. 284.

[74] "Hi quibus tantum humanis rebus et non divinis praeesse permissum est, quomodo de his, per quos divina ministrantur iudicare praesumant, paenitus ignoramus."—J. Mansi, *Sacrorum conciliorum nova et amplissima collectio* (53 vols., Parisiis, Arnheim, Lipsiae, 1901-1927), XV, 210. Hereafter this collection will be referred to as Mansi.

clerical immunity. In the Roman Synod of 1059, Pope Nicholas II (1059-1061) laid great stress on the idea of complete exemption of the clergy from lay jurisdiction.[75] The same concept was emphasized by Ivo of Chatres († c. 1116) in a letter to Wilgrin, the Archbishop of Paris,[76] and in a letter of Gregory VII (1073-1075) to Herrimanus, Bishop of Metz.[77] One important effect of the reform movement of Gregory was that the exemption of clerics from civil jurisdiction became more firmly established in ecclesiastical law. It was not until two centuries later, however, that guarantees for the complete exemption of the clergy *in their persons and in their goods* were incorporated into the statutes of civil law.

Article 4. The Concept of Clerical Immunity in the Decree of Gratian

In the decree of Gratian (1140 or shortly after)[78] the canons which relate to clerical immunity are scattered throughout the first and second books. It would be beyond the limits of this treatise to give a resumé of all these canons. It is sufficient to note, however, that this collection incorporated all the salient features of the preceeding legislation and formed the source for the opinion of the glossators regarding the juridical origin of clerical immunity. In the decree of Gratian are contained the *privilege of the canon,* which from canon 15 of the II General Council of the Lateran (1139) had universal force;[79] the admonition that bishops are not to be occupied with military affairs;[80] the argument of the glossator that, insofar as the servants of the churches, of the bishops and of the clergy are exempt from public duties, *a fortiori* the clergy themselves ought to be exempt

[75] Cc. 6 & 10—Mansi, XIX, 898.

[76] *MPL* CLXII, 140.

[77] VIII, 21—*MPL* CXLVIII, 594-601.

[78] Cf. S. Kuttner, "The Father of the Science of Canon Law,"—*The Jurist* (Published by the School of Canon Law: The Catholic University of America, Washington, D. C.), I (1940), p. 3 and note 2.

[79] C. 29, C. XVII, q. 4=c. 15, II Conc. Lateranensis—Mansi, XXI, 530.

[80] *Dictum* ad c. 19, C. XIII.

from these obligations;[81] and a statement of the principle that the Church can pay tribute out of goods which are not strictly *res sacrae*.[82] The exemption of the Church and the clergy from the obligation of paying taxes imposed by the civil authority had not yet reached its full stage of development.

Gratian devoted Question I of Causa XI to the matter of the privilege of the forum, and concluded that a cleric is not to be accused before a secular judge.[83] Although the regalists contended that Gratian had based his interpretation upon Pseudo-Isidore—and it is true that several of the canons in this section are excerpts from the Pseudo-Isidorian decretals—the contention is unfounded.[84] The decretals of Pope St. Nicholas I to the Emperor Michael III[85] and that of St. Gelasius I to the oriental bishops[86] are interesting for their interpretation by the glossator, in whose opinion the clergy were exempt from secular jurisdiction by divine law before any constitution to that effect existed,

[81] C. 69, C. XII, q. 2, with *dictum* and *glossa.*

[82] *"De suis exterioribus Ecclesia solvit tributum."*—c. 22, C. XXIII, q. 8. This canon is a *palea*—an insertion by Paucapalea († after 1148), the first commentator on the Decree. The text of this canon is ascribed to Pope Urban II (1088-1099), but is not found among his epistles. Berardi, however, is not inclined to consider it apocryphal; it is similar in tone to a letter sent by this pontiff to Robert, Count of Flanders, in protest against his rapacity against clerical property, which epistle is preserved among the acts of a synod held at Rheims in 1092—Harduin, *Acta Conciliorum,* VI, pars II, 1699.

[83] *Dictum* ad C. XI, q. 1.

[84] Cc. 1, 3, 9, 10, C. XI, q. 1 are Pseudo-Isidorian. These canons, however, are really *authentic* statements of law enacted by the councils of the sixth and seventh centuries whose text, as they appear in the Decree of Gratian, differs substantially from their original form. Pseudo-Isidore ascribed them to decretals of popes of an earlier time; but, as Cicognani observes, they introduced no new legislation.—*Canon Law* (authorized English version, 2. ed., revised by J. O'Hara and F. Brennan, Philadelphia: Dolphin Press, 1935), p. 247.

[85] *Supra,* p. 17 = c. 5, D. XCVI.

[86] *Supra,* p. 16 = c. 11, D. XCVI.

and that, consequently all constitutions which stated this principle were nothing more than declarations of divine law.[87]

[87] "Statuit Nicholaus, ut Imperator, qui tantum rebus humanis praesidet, se de rebus ecclesiasticis non intromittat nec de clericis iudicet." —*glossa* ad c. 5, D. XCVI.

"Ergo antequam esset aliqua constitutio, etiam clerici non erunt de iurisdictione saeculari: unde omnes constitutiones quae emanaverunt, quod clerici non sunt iudicandi nisi ab episcopis, non sunt nisi iuris [divini] declaratio."—*glossa* ad v. *et discuti,* c. 11, D. XCVI.

CHAPTER III

CLERICAL IMMUNITY FROM THE TWELFTH TO THE EIGHTEENTH CENTURY

In the legislation of the Decretals of Gregory IX (1234) which in its essentials remained the basic canon law until the Code (1918), the concept of clerical immunity was simply a complete lack of civil jurisdiction over the persons or over the goods of clerics. For two reasons the legislation of the decretals deserves special mention: in them the principle of clerical immunity was given the widest application, and at the time of the decretals—the period of the greatest influence of the Church in world affairs—the Church was better able to enforce the sanctions attached to clerical immunity than at any prior or subsequent period. Moreover, during this period guaranties for the observance of clerical immunity were incorporated into the civil law of the Holy Roman Empire.

ARTICLE 1. CLERICAL IMMUNITY IN THE DECRETAL LEGISLATION

Several noteworthy events preceeded the promulgation of the decretals, which conspired to establish firmly the principle of complete ecclesiastical and clerical immunity from secular jurisdiction. Among these were:

a) *The bitter contest between St. Thomas of Canterbury* († 1170) *and King Henry II of England* (1154-1189) over the latter's notion of what were the "ancient customs of the realm," as he outlined them in the "Constitutions of Clarendon" (1163).[1] This struggle culminated in the martyrdom of St. Thomas in the cause of the liberty and immunity of the Church.

b) *The III General Council of the Lateran* (1179) under Pope Alexander III (1159-1181). This Council threatened

[1] Mansi, XXI, 1187-1196; Hefele-LeClercq, *Histoire des Conciles d'apres les documents originaux* (10 vols. in 19, Paris, 1907-1938), V, nn. 623-630; J. Laux, *Church history* (New York: Benziger Brothers, 1935), pp. 338-340.

ex-communication against anyone who deliberately violated ecclesiastical jurisdiction by the imposition of any tax either upon the churches or upon churchmen without necessity and without the agreement of the clergy and their bishop.[2]

c) *A letter of Pope Innocent III* (1196-1216) *to the Emperor of Constantinople.* This letter influenced many later canonists in their attitude towards the basis of clerical immunity.[3]

d) *An important decision of Pope Innocent III.* In the adjudication of a dispute between the superior of the Monastery of St. Sylvester and the rector of the Church of Santa Maria in Via in Rome (1199), the pontiff clearly expressed the principle that lay persons have no jurisdiction over the churches or over ecclesiastical persons and that, even if their intervention be for the favor or utility of the Church, their action is simply invalid unless it is previously approved by the Church.[4]

e) *The action of the same pope at the IV General Council of the Lateran* (1215). Two of the decrees of this Council played a large part in the rather heated controversy between canonists and theologians over the precise juridical title of clerical immunity. These are the famous chapters *Nimis,*[5] which prohibited lay suzerains from demanding the oath of fealty of clerics, and *Non minus,* which added a further provision to the exemption from civil taxes and assessments upon the church or clergy—alienations of such property were not to be made for this purpose without the permission of the Holy See—and decreed that all sentences

[2] C. 19—Harduin, *Acta Conciliorum,* VI, pars II, 1681=c. 4, X, *de immunitate ecclesiarum, coemiterii et rerum ad eas pertinentium;* III, 49.

[3] "Imperium non praeest sacerdotio, sed subest, et ei obedire tenetur. Vel sic: Episcopus non debet subesse principibus sed praeesse."—Jaffé, *Regesta,* n. IX=c. 6, X, *de maioritate et obedientia,* I, 32.

[4] C. 10, X, *de constitutionibus,* I, 2.

[5] C. 14: "*Nimis de iure divino* quidem laici usurpare nituntur, quum viros ecclesiasticos, nihil temporale obtinentes ab eis, ad praestandum sibi fidelitatis iuramenta compellunt. Quia vero secundum apostolum servus suo domino stat aut cadat, sacri auctoritate concilii prohibemus, ne tales clerici personis saecularibus praestare cogantur huiusmodi iuramenta."—Harduin, *Acta Conciliorum,* VI, pars II, 52=c. 30, X, *de iureiurando,* II, 24.

and constitutions enacted by lay persons in this matter were *ipso iure* null and void.[6] Both of these decrees appealed to divine law as the basis of immunity, and both threatened excommunication against all who usurped ecclesiastical jurisdiction either by compelling the clergy to take the oath of fealty in lay courts or by imposing a tax upon the goods of the church or clergy.

f) Finally, *the incorporation of clerical immunity into civil law.* On the occasion of his coronation. Emperior Frederick II (1220-1250) issued a constitution in which he guaranteed that the liberty, jurisdiction and immunity of the Church and of the clergy would be observed throughout the Holy Roman Empire. Frederick incorporated three excerpts from this document into the civil code. These excerpts contained severe sanctions and were to be a warranty: 1. that all statutes contrary to the liberty of the Church or of the clergy were null and void; 2. that ecclesiastics were to be guaranteed the full privilege of the forum; and 3. that the fullest exemption from all public and private imposts, taxes and collections was to be accorded the clergy as well as to churches and other places of devotion.[7] This action marked a milestone in the history of clerical immunity.

These prescriptions of Frederick II were *received* into ecclesiastical law by Pope Honorius III (1216-1227), who praised them, admired the spirit in which they were written, and decreed that they were to remain in force forever.[8] The reception of clerical immunity into the civil law really added nothing to the *concept of the total exemption of the clergy and their goods from the secular authority;* this concept had been definitely determined by the enactments of the III General Council of the Lateran in 1179. The real importance of the laws of Frederick II lies in their ratification and "canonization" into ecclesiastical law by Pope Honorius III. This effectively answers the objection of the

[6] C. 46—Harduin, *Acta Conciliorum,* VII, pars II, 52=c. 7, X, *de immunitate ecclesiarum, coemiterii et rerum ad eas pertinentium, III,* 49.

[7] *Constitutiones et acta publica imperatorum et regum, Sectio IV* (8 toms., t. II, ed. L. Weiland, Hannoverae, 1896), n. 85, § 1-5, in *MGH.*

[8] Const., *"Has leges"—Fontes,* n. 31.

regalists that the concessions of Frederick II were mere privileges which could be revoked by the civil power at will.

The law of the decretals established that privileged jurisdiction over clerics was to admit of very few exceptions: all criminal cases of clerics, except those who had been declared incorrigible by an ecclesiastical judge, were to be tried only in the ecclesiastical forum, and no custom contrary to this privilege could prevail.[9] Essentially the legislation of the decretals indicates no great change from the laws prior to their promulgation; however, the decretals do not contain any *ex professo* statement regarding the juridical origin of clerical immunity. With regard to the exemption of the clergy from personal civic obligations which were incongruous with their sacred profession, the only legislation consists of the admonition that in time of great necessity the exemption of clerics cannot be urged, for at such times no one is excused from providing for the public safety.[10] With regard to the exemption of the clergy from civil taxes and exactions, the decretals simply restated the prescriptions of c. 19 of the III and c. 46 of the IV General Councils of the Lateran, which established the conditions under which the property of the Church and of clerics could be alienated for the aid of the State.[11] Moreover, in the decretals is recorded the first mention of the *"beneficium competentiae,"* by which a cleric cannot be pressed by his creditors to the extent that he would be without a decent measure of support. Although this privilege is not an exemption from civil law, inasmuch as the clergy can be convened only before an ecclesiastical judge, Ottaviani observes that it is considered an immunity insofar as it exempts from judicial action such portion of a cleric's goods which are necessary for his support.[12] As it stands in the decretals, the law protected an improvident cleric only against becoming subject to a sentence

[9] Cc. 1-17, X, *de iudiciis,* II, 1; cc. 1-10, X, *de foro competenti,* II, 2.

[10] C. 2, X, *de immunitate ecclesiarum, coemiterii et rerum ad eas pertinentium,* III, 49.

[11] Cc. 4 & 7, X, *de immunitate ecclesiarum, coemiterii et rerum ad eas pertinentium,* III, 49.

[12] *Institutiones iuris publici ecclesiastici,* I, 391.

of excommunication for the non-payment of his debts;[13] but from the beginning the privilege was given an extended interpretation to the effect that by virtue of it a cleric could not be imprisoned for the non payment of his debt, nor could he be deprived of such goods as were required for his decent support.

Article 2. Clerical Immunity and the Rise of Modern States

In its essential features the general law of the decretals remained unchanged until the eighteenth century. As yet the principle of ecclesiastical liberty had not been seriously challenged. Subsequently to the decretals, however, the very basis of clerical immunity—the right of the Church to remove her sacred ministers and their goods from secular jurisdiction—was bitterly attacked by the theories of Marsilius of Padua († 1342-1343) and his followers and by practices based on these theories by civil rulers who regarded the principle of clerical immunity as a violation of their natural rights. Henceforth the Church had to consolidate, defend and protect her liberty and independence of jurisdiction and its practical effects—the immunities of the clergy—from opposition both in theory and in practice, and to concede what could no longer be maintained without doing violence to the basis of clerical immunity. Papal protests against the curtailment of clerical immunity by the civil power are noted in the apostolic letters of Pope Gregory IX (1227-1241), Urban IV (1261-1264), Nicholas IV (1288-1292)[14] and particularly in the struggle between Pope Boniface VIII (1294-1303) and King Philip IV of France (1285-1314).

[13] C. 3, X, *de solutionibus*, III, 23; cf. c. 16, X, *de restitutione spoliatorum*, III, 13.

[14] Const. *"Rex qui regni,"* 19 feb. 1236—Roskovány, *Monumenta Catholica pro independentia potestatis ecclesiasticae ab imperio civili* (13 vols., Quinque Ecclesiis [Fünfkirchen] et Nitriae, 1847-1879, n. 138; Litt. ap. *"Quamvis sit,"* 12 iun. 1263—*Bullarium romanum,* III. 696; Litt. ap. *"Provisionis nostrae,"* 1 dec. 1263—*Bullarium romanum,* III, 700; Litt. ap. *"Dudum ad nostrum,"* 25 maii 1282—Roskovány, *Monumenta Catholica,* n. 421.

The *Liber Sextus* of Boniface VIII (1298) developed many ramifications and applications of the principle of clerical immunity and in vigorous language castigated those who presumed to violate it,[15] although indirectly Boniface restricted the privilege of the forum by excluding from its benefit those for whom it was no longer strictly necessary.[16] Moreover the *Liber Sextus* incorporated the decrees on immunity which had been promulgated since the time of Gregory IX,[17] and embodied the first of several explicit statements regarding the *juridical origin* of ecclesiastical and clerical immunity:

> **Cum igitur ecclesiae ecclesiasticaeque personae ac res ipsarum non solum a iure humano sed et divino a saecularibus personarum exactionibus sint immunes . . .** [18]

Advertence to these chapters is of the utmost importance in order to understand the concept of complete exemption of the clergy and their goods from the power of civil authority by reason of an absolute lack of civil jurisdiction over the clergy. It must be remembered that the protests of Pope Boniface VIII in these as well as in other letters [19] during his struggle with Philip the Fair represent a thorny situation *as it existed in fact:* it would have been beside the point to protest merely against the

[15] C. 2, *de foro competenti*, II, 2, in VI°; cf. c. 2, *de officio et potestate iudicis delegati*, I, 24, in VI°; c. 2, *de sententia et re iudicata*, II, 14, in VI°; cc. 2, 12, 15, 21, 23, *de sententia excommunicationis, suspensionis et interdicti*, V, 11, in VI°.

[16] C. 1, *de clericis coniugatis*, III, 2, in VI°.

[17] Cc. 1 & 3, *de immunitate ecclesiarum, coemiteriorum et aliorum locorum religiosorum*, III, 23, in VI°. C. 3 of this title is the famous Bull "*Clericis laicos*" (1 mar. 1296), which augmented the already severe legislation of the III and IV General Councils of the Lateran.

[18] C. 4, *de censibus, exactionibus, et procurationibus*, III, 20, in VI°.

[19] Epist. "*Ineffabilis amoris,*" 26 sept. 1296—Roskovány, *Monumenta Catholica*, n. 422; Epist. "*Verba delirantis,*"—Roskovány, *Monumenta Catholica*, n. 425; Const. "*Unam sanctam,*" 18 nov. 1302—Denzinger, *Enchiridion*, nn. 468-469, cf. also c. 1, *de maioritate et obedientia*, in Extravag. comm., I, 8.

violation of clerical immunity when *in practice* native rights of the Church and of the clerical order were openly disregarded by the King of Francc. Moreover, it was necessary for the pope to recall that the right of the Church to establish immunities is a divine right and that the complete exemption of the clergy and their goods from any obligation that could be imposed under the title of jurisdiction by the civil power had already been guaranteed in both ecclesiastical and civil law. With theese facts in mind, the words of Boniface that immunities are of divine as well as of human law, can be properly evaluated. The problem which has confronted the Church from the days of Boniface VIII until the present time has been the necessity of protesting against actions by secular powers which are abuses of both divine and human law. The point at issue was the need of safeguarding the liberty of the Church and of protecting it against the usurpation of ecclesiastical jurisdiction by the lay power. This is the basis of immunity, and immunities are the corollaries, exemplifications, and guarantees of ecclesiastical liberty.

The severe provisions of the two famous Bulls of Pope Boniface VIII—the *Clericis laicos* and the *Unam sanctum* were mollified by the conciliatory legislation of Pope Clement V (1305-1314) on account of the "scandals, grave difficulties and hardships to which their provisions had given rise," and because Clement feared that they would be "the occasion of greater scandals, difficulties and hardships in the future;" and the *status quo ante* was restored.[20] Pope John XXII (1316-1334), the successor of Clement V, was faced with even more pressing problems, chief among which were a bitter contest with the Emperor Louis of Bavaria and the rise of the theories of William of Occam († 1349-1350), Marsilius of Padua and others.[21] The struggle between Boniface VIII and Philip IV of France, however, is of singular importance because it represents the difficult

[20] C. 2, V, 7, *de privilegiis,* in Extravag. comm.; c. un., *de immunitate ecclesiarum,* III, 17 in Clem.

[21] P. Albers, *Enchiridion historiae ecclesiasticae universae* (3. ed., 3 vols., Neomagii in Hollandia, 1910), II, 280-284.

period of transition between the middle ages and the rise of the modern State.

Article 3. Clerical Immunity From the Fifteenth to the Eighteenth Century

Notwithstanding the condemnation of the theories of Marsilius of Padua and others by Pope John XXII,[22] various factors were at work between the fourteenth and the eighteenth centuries to foster the theory of State-absolutism. The confusion caused by the residence of the popes at Avignon (1309-1377) and by the "Great Western Schism" (1378-1417) gave rise to a diminution of papal influence and afforded impetus to a program of systematic violation of the liberty of the Church and to the usurpation of her jurisdiction by lay powers, based upon the secularist theories of Marsilius. This program implied a direct negation of the exclusive jurisdiction of the Church over clerics and their goods. Within the Church this spirit was represented by Gallicanism or Regalism in various forms and under different names; outside the Church Protestantism gave full reign to the theories of Marsilius of Padua. To resist these attacks vigorous measures were taken by the Holy See. Special mention should be made regarding the attempts of Pope Martin V (1417-1431), of Pope Leo X (1513-1521) and of the Council of Trent (1545-1563) to uphold the principle of complete ecclesiastical and clerical immunity from the jurisdiction of the civil powers.

Pope Martin V made it clear that not withstanding the utter incompetence of lay persons over the goods or over the persons of ecclesiastics, there were some who persisted in violating this immunity and in usurping ecclesiastical jurisdiction. He provided severe canonical sanctions against all who presumed to continue these practices.[23] Two Constitutions of Pope Leo X, promulgated at the V General Council of the Lateran (1512-

[22] Const. *"Licet iuxta,"—Fontes,* n. 38; cf. also Denzinger, *Enchiridion Symbolorum,* nn. 493 & 499.

[23] Const. *"Ad evitanda,"* (a. 1418)—*Fontes,* n. 45; Const. *"Ad reprimendas,"* 1 feb. 1428, §§ 1-4, *Fontes,* n. 46.

1517), further illustrate the fact that, despite the pretensions of the civil powers, the papacy continued to strive with all its zeal to maintain the realization of complete ecclesiastical exemption from civil jurisdiction in all its pristine vigor. In both these Constitutions[24] the Pontiff deplored the serious violations of ecclesiastical liberty and immunity, protested against the obsequiousness of those members of the clergy who cooperated in these violations and renewed the laws of his predecessors which provided the penalty of excommunication *ipso facto* against those who offended against the principle of complete exemption of clergymen and their goods from lay jurisdiction. In the Constitution *Supernae dispositionis* Leo made use of the identical words of Boniface VIII regarding the juridical origin of clerical immunity:

> **Et cum a iure, tam divino quam humano, Laicis potestas nulla in Ecclesiasticis personas attributa sit . . .**[25]

The Council of Trent (1545-1563) enacted two important decrees which affected clerical immunity. The *first* reduced the number of those who could enjoy the privilege of the forum by adding to the conditions already laid down by Boniface VIII[26] others which effectively excluded from the enjoyment of the privilege those for whom it was not necessary;[27] the *second* recalled to secular powers their obligation to defend the clergy and the property of the Church against all who attacked their liberty, immunity and jurisdiction, and added another significant statement regarding the *juridical origin* of immunity:

> **Ecclesiae et personarum ecclesiasticarum immunitatem Dei ordinatione et canonicis sanctionibus constitutam.**[28]

[24] Leo X (in Conc. Lateranen.), const., *"Supernae dispositionis,"* 5 maii 1514—*Fontes,* n. 65; const. *"Regimini universalis,"* 4 maii 1515—*Fontes,* n. 66.

[25] *Fontes,* n. 65.

[26] C. 1, *de clericis coniugatis,* III, 2, in VI°; cf. *supra,* p. 26.

[27] Sess. XXIII, *de ref.,* c. 8.

[28] Sess. XXV, *de ref.,* c. 20.

The Fathers of the Council of Trent solemnly recalled to secular princes all the sanctions whereby ecclesiastical and clerical immunity were protected, repeated the admonition that immunities existed by virtue of divine ordinance as well as by canonical sanctions, reviewed the all too frequent violations of ecclesiastical immunity in the past, and expressed the fervent hope that in the future—with the cooperation of Christian princes in this matter—clerics would be enabled to exercise their divine office in peace and without hindrance and thereby secure more fruitful and more edifying results from their labors. The decree spoke of clerical immunity in general, in the broad sense of the term. At least in respect to the *basis* of immunity or the right of the Church, as a perfect society independent of and superior to the State, to exempt her clergy from civil jurisdiction, together with the *motive* that God be better served, immunity can rightly be said to be of divine as well as of human law. In this sense the words of the Council are a repetition of those of Popes Leo X,[29] Martin V,[30] Boniface VIII,[31] Gregory IX,[32] Honorius III,[33] Innocent III,[34] Alexander III,[35] Gregory VII,[36] Nicholas II,[37] Nicholas I,[38] Gregory I,[39] Gelasius I,[40] Leo I,[41] and of St.

[29] Const. *"Supernae dispositionis,"* 5 maii 1514—*Fontes,* n. 65; cf. *supra,* p. 29.

[30] Const. *"Ad reprimendas,"* 1 feb. 1428—*Fontes,* n. 46; cf. *supra,* p. 28.

[31] C. 4, *de censibus, exactionibus et procurationibus,* III, 20, in VI°; cf. *supra,* p. 26.

[32] C. 10, X, *de constitutionibus,* I, 2; c. 8, X, *de iudiciis,* I. 2; cc. 1-5, X, *de foro competenti,* II, 2; cc. 4 & 7, X, *de immunitate ecclesiarum, coemiterii et rerum ad eas pertinentium,* III, 49; cf. *supra,* pp. 22-24.

[33] Const. *"Has leges,"* a 1220—*Fontes,* n. 31; cf. *supra,* p. 23.

[34] C. 10, X, *de constitutionibus,* I, 2; cf. *supra,* p. 22.

[35] Cc. 14 & 19, III Conc. Lateranen.—Harduin, *Acta Conciliorum,* VI, pars II, 1679 & 1681; cf. *supra,* pp. 23-24.

[36] Letter to Herrimanus (lib. VII, ep. 21)—*MPL* CXLVIII, 594-601; cf. *supra,* p. 18.

[37] Cc. 6 & 10, Roman Synod of 1059—Mansi, XIX, 898; cf. *supra,* p. 18.

[38] Mansi, XV, 210=c. 5, D. XCVI; cf. *supra,* p.

[39] Lib. IX, epp. 203-204; lib. XIII, epp. 47, 49, 50; lib. XI, ep. 24; cf. *supra,* pp. 16-17.

Ambrose [42] and St. Hilary.[43]

In the writings of the Fathers and in the decrees of the pontiffs and councils the term *ecclesiastical immunity* had been employed without any restriction between strictly spiritual and ecclesiastical matters on the one hand, and civil and criminal causes and temporal matters in general on the other. Notwithstanding the recourse of clergymen themselves to the lay power, and despite flagrant violations of immunity along with the usurpation of jurisdiction that was not their own by secular princes, the Church has ever upheld her native and exclusive competence in all these matters. It is in this broad sense of the term, and prescinding from the distinction between the sacred and the civil character of priests, that the word immunity has consistently been employed in the legislation of the Church.

In order to protect and defend ecclesiastical immunity and jurisdiction, Pope Urban VIII (1623-1644) found it necessary to establish the *Sacred Congregation of Ecclesiastical Immunity* on June 22, 1626. This Congregation issued many decrees, although no official collection of acts was ever compiled. After the invasion of Rome in 1870, the work of this body was restricted to the Papal States, inasmuch as such conflicts that arose regarding clerical immunity were provided for by direct action between the Papal Secretariat of State and the heads of the various nations, usually in *concordats*. In his reorganization of the Roman Curia in 1908, Pope Pius X (1903-1914) suppressed this Congregation.

In addition to the legislation seen thus far, another important papal document is worthy of notice. This was the Bull *Coenae*, or *in Coena Domini*. The bull took its title from the fact that it was solemnly read each year at Rome on Holy Thursday, between

[40] Epist. XV, cap. 10=c. 12, C. XI, q. 1; *Bullarium Romanum, appendix*, n. 306=c. 13, C. XI, q. 1. Gratian had attributed the excerpt from epist. XV, cap. 10, to a certain Pope John [VIII?]. It is in fact a word for word restatement of the letter of St. Gelasius to the Oriental bishops.

[41] Epist. LIII—*MPL*, LIV, 657; cf. *supra*, p. 15.

[42] *MPL*, XVI, 592; cf. *supra*, p. 12.

[43] *MPL*, X, 557; cf. *supra*, p. 12.

the years 1364 and 1700. It assumed various forms between the time of its first promulgation by Pope Urban V (1362-1370) and its final revision in 1627 by Urban VIII (1623-1644). This document contained the list of censures reserved *speciali modo* to the Holy See.

After 1657 it was read in other places outside Rome as well; although efforts to publish it solemnly in every part of the world were foiled by strong opposition from secular governments. In Austria, Emperor Joseph II (1765-1790) decreed that it be suppressed; and its reading was specifically forbidden by the civil authorities in France, Portugal and other countries.[44]

It is commonly held that the provisions of this bull remained in force until the Constitution *"Apostolicae Sedis,"* which was issued by Pope Pius IX on October 12, 1879, supplanted all earlier penal legislation that was of a general character and of universal binding force.

Five of the twenty censures mentioned in the Bull *in Coena Domini* concerned ecclesiastical immunity, to wit: § 13, appeals from ecclesiastical to lay courts; § 14, the cession of spiritual cases to lay courts; § 15, the subjection of ecclesiastics to lay courts; § 18, the imposition of tithes or taxes by the lay power upon the clergy without the special permission of the Holy See; and § 19, the interference of lay judges in capital criminal cases of bishops.[45]

[44] *Catholic Encyclopedia,* I, 647; VII, 717-718.

[45] The text of the Bull *in Coena Domini* as read during the pontificates of Popes Alexander VI (1655-1667), Paul V (1605-1621), and Gregory XIV (1590-1591), together with very detailed commentaries on the same are contained in L. Duardo, *Commentaria* in Bullam S.D.N.D. Pauli Quinti lectam in die coenae domini anno MDCXVIII *in die coenae domini anno MDCXVIII in tres libros distincta* (Mediolani, 1620); D. Ambrosio, *Commentaria in bullam Greg. XIV de immunitate et libertate ecclesiastica* (4. ed., Bracciani, 1633); J. Fatolillus, *Theatrum immunitatis et liberatatis ecclesiasticae* (2 vols., Romae, 1714), text on pp. 395-405.

Chapter IV

CLERICAL IMMUNITY FROM THE EIGHTEENTH CENTURY TO THE CODE

The eighteenth and nineteenth centuries saw the breach between Church and State growing wider than hitherto. In Italy, Germany, Austria and France, as well as in the Central and South American republics, the movement to subdue the Church and to subject her to secular control continued with renewed vigor. Under the names of Gallicanism, Regalism, Febronianism, Josephinism and other so called "liberal" theories, anticlericalism was rampant.[1] The most potent movement in disturbing the relationship between Church and State during this period was the French Revolution (1789), which brought about a complete separation of Church and State,[2] and sinned not only against the immunities but against the very concept of the freedom and independence of the Church from the lay power as well.

The Holy See met the challenge of secularism in a twofold way: 1. the popes denounced the excesses of civil governments for their violations of the rights of the Church and of the clergy, condemned in particular the usurpation of her proper and native jurisdiction by the lay power, and sternly recalled to all the true principles which govern the mutual rights and duties of Church and State. 2. In concordats with the various nations, the Holy See in practice allowed concessions which *in fact* amounted to a validation of what had been usurpations by the civil power; and was content to accept guaranties for the preservation of the dignity of clerics in their arrest, detention, conviction and punishment by the civil governments for offenses against the civil law;

[1] S. Aicher, *Compendium iuris ecclesiastici* (6. ed., Brixiae, 1887), nn. 43-44; Wernz, *Ius decretalium,* I, 34-45; F. Cavagnis, *Institutiones iuris publici ecclesiastici,* II, 45-56; P. Albers, *Enchiridion,* III, 224-306; F. Cappello, *Summa iuris publici ecclesiastici,* pp. 166-178; M. Conte a Coronata, *Ius publicum ecclesiasticum,* 131.

[2] P. Albers, *Enchiridion,* III, 247-250; Wernz, *Ius decretalium,* I, 42; Cappello, *Summa iuris publici ecclesiastici,* 372-373.

and—in some cases by express provision, in others by tacit acquiescence to contrary secular legislation—no longer urged her former severe sanctions against certain actions by secular governments that would be offensive to the idea of a complete lack of jurisdiction on the part of the civil power over the persons or over the temporal goods of the clergy.[3]

In the concordats it was clearly stated that in regard to coercive jurisdiction concessions were made to civil governments not as a matter of principle, but merely in view of the exigencies of the times. The concordats, however, are worthy of note for their silence in regard to some features of clerical exemption, as well as for their expressions which indicate that the full concept of exemption of the clergy from civil jurisdiction was no longer urged.

Article 1. The Action of the Holy See in Concordats

In order to effect a *modus vivendi* between Church and State during the eighteenth and nineteenth centuries and to safeguard the rights of the Church, the Holy See found it necessary to enter into pacts or concordats with the various nations. An analysis of these concordats indicates that it was no longer possible or necessary to maintain all the ample ramifications implied in the notion of a complete exemption of the clergy and their goods from any obligation that could be imposed under the title of civil jurisdiction. As Wernz observes, the concessions allowed by the Holy See in the concordats amounted to a sanation of what had been violations of immunity and usurpations of ecclesiastical jurisdiction which, until these had been ratified by the Holy See, had been merely tolerated in order that greater evils might be avoided.[4]

[3] "Item principes civiles sunt vere fontes iuris in illis causis clericorum de bonis privatis quae ex iure tantum humano exclusive olim foro canonico fuerunt reservatae; nunc vero propter abrogatam legem canonicam denuo sub nativa et propria potestate legifera principum saecularium sunt constitutae."—Wernz, *Ius decretalium,* I, 300.

[4] "Quo in casu istae leges nequaquam vi legum civilium obligant, sed ex necessitate vitandi maiora mala et ex voluntate ecclesiae. Tandem non

The almost complete silence of the concordats regarding any exemption of the private goods of the clergy from taxation by the civil authority is sufficient indication that the Holy See recognized that this particular immunity is no longer feasible in view of the changed conditions of modern society. In only four concordats was mention made of this matter at all, and these explicitly stated that the clergy and their possessions were to be subjected to public taxes in the same manner as were the persons and goods of other citizens.[5] Prior to the Code, little mention was made in concordats regarding the exemption of clerics from public office. It was to be expected that, with the rise of liberalism, the exclusion of clerics from public office by secular powers was motivated not by respect for the divine vocation of the clergy, but rather by the desire of the liberalists to thwart their influence in society.[6]

By far the greater amount of consideration regarding clerical immunity in the concordats was given to the question of the competence of lay judges over the contentious and criminal cases of clerics. These provided that wherever the immunity of clerics from the jurisdiction of civil courts could be upheld, although within narrower limits than heretofore, it was to be guaranteed.[7] Thus, in some concordats it was provided that the ecclesiastical

raro, Romanus Pontifex, quod ab initio per iniustas leges civiles usurpatum fuerat, concessione indulti vel privilegii concordatis sanat."—*Ius decretalium,* I, 296.

[5] Art. 7-8, *Concordat between Clement XII* (1730-1740) *and Philip V of Spain* (1737)—V. Nussi, *Conventiones de rebus ecclesiasticis inter S. Sedem et civilem potestatem variis formis initae ex collectione romana excerptae* (Monguntiae, 1870), n. IX (Hereafter this work will be referred to as *Conventiones); Concordat between Benedict XIV* (1740-1758) *and Charles Emmanuel III, King of Sardinia* (1742)—*Conventiones,* n. *XII;* art. 10, *Concordat between the Holy See and Sicily* (1818)—*Conventiones,* n. XXV; *Concordat between the Holy See and Equador* (1862) —*Conventiones,* n. XLVII.

[6] F. Cavagnis, *Institutiones iuris publici ecclesiastici,* II, 179; F. Cappello, *Summa iuris publici ecclesiastici,* p. 472.

[7] Cappello, *Summa,* pp. 466-467; Ottaviani, *Institutiones,* II, 394-395; Coronata, *Ius publicum ecclesiasticum,* p. 200.

forum was to be retained, although for certain cases in which clerics figured mixed tribunals were established.[8] Where it was possible, provision was made that cases between clerics be tried before an ecclesiastical judge, although *merely civil caess* of the clergy were to be heard before a lay judge.[9] For the greater part however, the right of the ecclesiastical forum in criminal matters was ignored by secular governments, and in practice the Holy See was content, although only "in view of the exigencies of the times," to accept agreements that certain definite guarantees were to be observed by the civil powers to maintain the reverence due to the clerical state in the arrest, conviction, detention and punishment of clerics who had been accused or convicted on criminal charges. The insistence of the Holy See upon such guarantees is a strong indication of the reluctance of the Church to allow derogation from her proper jurisdiction over the criminal cases of her clergy. The special provisions which were incorporated into the concordats were not the same in each case; but in their broader provisions they represented such practical safeguards of clerical dignity as the Holy See was able to demand in its relations with each nation.[10]

That the provisions of the concordats were not universally respected by the various nations is evident from many documents

[8] E.g., *Concordats between the Holy See and Sicily* (1741), and *Sardinia* (1742)—Nussi, *Conventiones,* nn. XII-XIII.

[9] Art. 12, *Concordat between Pius VII* (1800-1823) *and Maximilian of Bavaria* (1817)—Nussi, *Conventiones,* n. XXII.

[10] Artt. 1-2, *Pact between Gregory XVI* (1831-1846) *and Frederick II, King of both Sicilies* (1834); Artt. 1 & 3, *Conventione sull' immunità ecclesiastica personale* (1841) *between the same pontiff and Charles Albert, King of Sardinia*—Nussi, *Conventiones,* nn. XXXII & XXXIV; Art. 10, *Pact between Pius IX* (1846-1878) *and Leopold III, Grand Duke of Etruria* (1851)—Nussi, *Conventiones,* n. XXXVII; artt. 13-14, *Concordat between Pius IX and Franz Joseph I, Emperor of Austria* (1855),—Nussi, *Conventiones,* n. XLI; artt. 14-15, *Concordat between the Holy See and Costa Rica* (1852)—Nussi, *Conventiones,* n. XXXIX; artt. 15-16, *Concordat with Guatamala* (1852)—Nussi, *Conventiones,* XL; Artt. 14-15, *Concordat with San Salvador* (1862)—Nussi *Conventiones,* n. LI; *Concordat with Venezuela* (1862)—Nussi, *Conventiones,* n. XLIX; *Concordat with Equador* (1862)—Nussi, *Conventiones,* n. XLVII.

of the Holy See, especially from the condemnation in the *Syllabus errorum* (1864) of the proposition:

> Laica potestas auctoritatem habet rescindendi, declarandi ac faciendi irritas solemnes conventiones (vulgo *concordata*) super usu iurium ad ecclesiasticam immunitatem pertinentium cum Sede Apostolica initas sine huius consensu, immo et ea reclamante.[11]

Since the promulgation of the Code, derogations from the *privileged forum* of the clergy have been made expressly by the Holy See upon the agreement of secular governments to observe certain conditions and definite safeguards to protect the dignity of the clerical state.[12] In the Concordat with Latvia, clerics in major orders are declared exempt from military service and from other civic functions incompatible with the priestly vocation;[13] in the concordats with other nations other special provisions are made for ecclesiastics. They are exempt from certain definite civic functions incompatible with the vocation to the priesthood, and in some countries from military service as well, except in time of general mobilization.[14]

Article 2. Statements of the Holy See

During the period from the eighteenth century to the Code the Holy See on several occasions found it necessary to condemn in most vigorous terms the action of civil governments, not only in violation of clerical immunity, but in the usurpation of ecclesias-

[11] Prop. 43—Denzinger, *Enchiridion Symbolorum,* n. 1743.

[12] *Concordat with Latvia* (May 30, 1922), artt. XVII, XVIII, XIX—Perugini, *Concordata vigentia* (Romae: apud custodiam librariam Pont. instituti utriusque iuris, 1934), p. 7; *Concordat with Lithuania* (Sept. 27, 1927), art. XX—*Concordata vigentia,* p. 67; *Concordat with Poland* (Feb. 10, 1925), art. XX—*Concordata vigentia,* pp. 43-44; *Concordat with Italy* (Feb. 21, 1929), art. 8—*Concordata vigentia,* p. 117; *Concordat with Austria* (June 5, 1933), art. XX—*Concordata vigentia,* pp. 293-294.

[13] Art. IX—Concordata vigentia, p. 5.

[14] Particular provisions are outlined in the *Concordat with Poland,* art. V—*Concordata vigentia,* p. 12; in the *Concordat with Lithuania,* art. V—*Concordata vigentia,* p. 61; in the *Concordat with Italy,* art. 3—*Concordata vigentia,* p. 99;

tical jurisdiction in other matters as well. Pope Clement XIII (1758-1769) bitterly complained against violations of ecclesiastical liberty and jurisdiction in regard to the forum of the clergy in Prussia.[15] Pius IX (1846-1878) was constrained in 1848 to denounce a law enacted by the government of Sardinia, which abolished clerical immunity in definance of the Concordat.[16] That this reproof did not have its desired effect is evident from another allocution in regard to the same matter ten years later.[17] The essential note of these two protests was embodied in the *Syllabus errorum,* wherein Pius IX condemned the proposition that the lay power has the right to declare null and void solemn pacts in the matter of ecclesiastical immunity into which it had entered with the Holy See.[18]

In the apostolic letter *Multiplices inter,* Pius condemned the liberal opinions expressed by Francis Vigil, a priest in Peru, and repeated the language of the Council of Trent in his condemnation of Vigil's teachings:

> Ecclesiae et personarum ecclesiasticarum immunitatem Dei ordinatione et canonicis sanctionibus constitutam, a iure civili ortum habuisse asserit [Vigil].[19]

This proposition, too, was incorporated into the *Syllabus errorum:*

> Ecclesiae et personarum ecclesiasticarum immunitas a iure civili ortum habuit.[20]

The pontiff again found it necessary to protest against the violations of the rights of religion and ecclesiastical liberty in the Republic of Columbia[21] and in Mexico.[22] Not the least of these

[15] Clemens XIII, epist. encycl. "*Cum a multo,*" 18 dec. 1762—*Fontes,* n. 458.

[16] Pius IX, alloc. "*In consistoriali*" 1 nov. 1850, § 3—*Fontes,* n. 509.

[17] Alloc. "*Multis gravibusque,*" 17 dec. 1860, § 2—*Fontes,* n. 529.

[18] Prop. 43—Denzinger, *Enchiridion Symbolorum,* n. 1743; cf. *supra,* p. 37.

[19] Litt. ap. "*Multiplices inter,*" 10 iun. 1851, § 3—*Fontes,* n. 510.

[20] Prop. 30—Denzinger, *Enchiridion Symbolorum,* n. 1730.

[21] Alloc. "*Acerbissimum,*" 27 sept. 1852, § 1—*Fontes,* n. 515.

[22] Alloc. "*Numquam fore,*" 15 dec. 1856, § 5—*Fontes,* 522.

violations and usurpations was the summary abolition of the privileged forum of the clergy by secularist governments. The attitude of liberal politicians who attempted to justify this abuse on the plea of the equality of all citizens before the law was again condemned by the incorporation of the following proposition into the *Syllabus:*

> Ecclesiasticum forum pro temporalibus clericorum causis sive civilibus sive criminalibus omnino de medio tollendum est, etiam inconsulta et reclamante Apostolica Sede.[23]

Especially since the latter half of the last century the application of the concept of clerical immunity to the exemption of the clergy from military service has been seriously threatened by the liberals.[24] The theories of the liberals were put into practice in the civil laws of Austria, Hungary, Prussia, Italy and France, and clerics were forced to undertake military service; only such exemptions were granted which the governments designed to make in favor of *certain classes* of clergymen.[25] That the Holy See made vigorous protest against this violation of natural right and equity is evident from the strong language employed by Pope Pius IX in a letter to the Archbishop of Monreale, in Sicily,[26]

[23] Prop. 31—Denzinger, *Enchiridion Symbolorum,* n. 1731.

[24] Wernz, *Ius decretalium,* II, 238; Cavagnis, *Institutiones iuris publici ecclsiastici,* II, 179; Cappello, *Summa iuris publici ecclesiastici,* pp. 468-471; Coronata, *Ius publicum ecclesiasticum,* pp. 216-219; Ottaviani, *Institutiones iuris publici ecclesiastici,* I, 395; Vermeersch-Creusen, *Epitome iuris canonici,* I, 213.

[25] The details of these laws can be found in Aichner, *Compendium iuris ecclesiastici,* pp. 236-237 and note 23. Cf. also Vermeersch-Creusen and Ottaviani, *locc. citt.*

[26] "Iniquissimam esse legem, qua clerici militari conquisitioni subiiciantur . . . sacrisque ministris per summam iniustitiam et impietatem illata pergat maiore in dies audacia ac diabolico prorsus furore et odio in Ecclesiam modis omnibus insectandi. Nos igitur eamdem infandam legem de clericis in militiam adscribendis Ecclesiae libertati ac immunitati maxime adversam, ac rei Catholicae et ipsi civili societati perniciosam iam nunc reprobamus, damnamus, quoties lex ipsa quovis modo fuerit sancita."—25 mar. 1869, Roskovàny, *Monumenta Catholica,* n. 2367.

and in the incorporation into the *Syllabus* of the proposition that the exemption of the clergy from military service can be abrogated by the State, and that civil progress, especially in a liberal form of government, demands its abrogation:

> Absque ulla naturalis iuris et aequitatis violatione potest abrogari personalis immunitas qua clerici ab onere subeundae exercendaeque militiae eximuntur; hanc vero abrogationem postulat civilis progressus, maxime in societate ad formam liberioris regiminis constituta.[27]

Other protests against this form of violation of clerical immunity were made by the same pontiff,[28] by Pope Leo XIII (1875-1903)[29] and by Pope Pius X (1903-1914).[30]

That the Holy See remained firm in its purpose to maintain personal clerical immunity, except insofar as had been provided otherwise in the concordats, is evident from the censures provided in the Constitution *Apostolicae Sedis* of Pius IX. This Constitution renewed the *latae sententiae* excommunication—which for its absolution was reserved *speciali modo* to the Holy See—against those who constrained lay judges in contravention of canonical ordinances to cite ecclesiastical persons before their tribunal, or who issue laws or decrees contrary to the liberty or rights of the Church.[31] It likewise renewed the *latae sententiae* excommunication—which for its absolution was *simpliciter* reserved to the Holy See—against those who laid violent hands upon the person of a cleric or a religious.[32] Even after the promulga-

[27] Prop. 32—Denzinger, *Enchiridion Symbolorum*, n. 1732.

[28] Alloc. "*Luctuosis exagitati*," 12 mar. 1877, § 1—*Fontes*, n. 572.

[29] Epist. "*Da grave*," 27 aug. 1878—*Fontes*, n. 575.

[30] S. C. de Religiosis decr., "*Inter reliquas*," 1 ian. 1911—*Fontes*, n. 4408.

[31] Pius IX, const. "*Apostolicae Sedis*," 12 oct. 1860, § I, n. 7: "Cogentes sive directe, sive indirecte, iudices laicos ad trahendum ad suum tribunal personas ecclesiasticas praeter canonicas dispositiones: item edentes leges vel decreta contra libertatem aut iura ecclesiae."—*Fontes*, n. 552. The present legislation in this matter is contained in c. 2334.

[32] *Ibid.*, n. 2: "Violentas manus, suadente diabolo, iniicientes in Clericos, vel utriusque sexus Monachos, exceptis quoad reservationem casibus et personis, de quibus iure vel privilegio permittitur, ut Episcopus aut alius absolvat." The present legislation is contained in c. 2343.

tion of the *Apostolicae Sedis* it was necessary for the pope to protest against the violation of the rights of the Church and of the clergy in Switzerland [33] and in Prussia.[34]

With regard to the application of the word *cogentes* (Const. *Apostolicae Sedis,* § n. 7) the question was raised whether the excommunication was to be applied only to legislators and other public personages, or was to be extended to all who would compel a member of the clergy to appear before a lay tribunal. In response to this difficulty, the Sacred Congregation of the Holy Office replied that only legislators and other public persons were subject to the *ipso facto* excommunication reserved *speciali modo* to the Holy See, that this declaration was approved and confirmed by the pope, and was to be communicated to all local ordinaries.[35] Nevertheless a new law was enacted twenty-five years later, in the *motu proprio "Quantavis diligentia,"* which made the case more inclusive. In this *motu proprio* Pope Pius X solemnly affirmed that the censure would henceforth be incurred by all persons who were guilty of violation of the privileged forum of the clergy.[36]

The present law regarding the privileged forum of the clergy can be summed up in the following manner: 1. It establishes the native and exclusive competence of the Church to try all contentious or criminal cases of the clergy, religious of either sex and their novices, and also members of pious societies who live in common without vows;[37] 2. It decrees that clerics in all conten-

[33] Epist. encycl. *"Etsi multa,"* 21 nov. 1873, §§ 1-8—*Fontes,* n. 566.

[34] *Ibid.,* §§ 9-19.

[35] S.C.S.Off., litt. encycl., 23 ian. 1886—*Fontes,* 1099.

[36] "Itaque hoc Nos Motu Proprio statuimus atque edicimus: quicumque privatorum, laici sacrive ordinis, mares feminaeve, personas quasvis ecclesiasticas, sive in criminali causa sive in civili, nullo potestatis ecclesiasticae permissu, ad tribunal laicorum vocent, ibique adesse publice compellant, eos etiam omnes in Excommunicationem latae sententiae speciali modo Romano Pontifici reservatam incurrere.

"Quod autem his litteris sancitum est, firmum ratumque esse volumus, contrariis quibusvis non obstantibus."—Motu proprio *"Quantavis diligentia,"* 9 oct. 1911—*Fontes,* n. 694.

[37] Canon 1553, § 1, 3°.

tious or criminal cases be convened before an ecclesiastical judge unless some other provision has legitimately been made for particular places.[38] They cannot be convened before a lay judge *without the license of the Holy See*—in the case of certain dignitaries—*or of the local ordinary*—in the case of all others who enjoy the privilege of the forum;[39] although if they are convened by one who has neglected to obtain proper authorization, they can appear in court nevertheless, because of necessity and in order to avoid greater difficulties. In this case, however, the superior from whom license should have been obtained is to be acquainted with the facts.[40] 3. The present law provides penal sanctions for the violation of these prescriptions.[41] This legislation is milder than that of the *motu proprio* of Pius X.

Article 3. The Force of Custom Contrary to Immunity

A word must be added here regarding the force of custom in the derogation of clerical immunity. The necessity of legal consent on the part of the legislator is at least a condition *sine qua non* for the valid introduction of a custom.[42] This represents no change from the old law.[43] Moreover, no custom can be admitted

[38] Canon 120, § 1.

[39] Canon 120, § 2.

[40] Canon 120, § 3.

[41] The reservation of the censure of excommunication *speciali modo* or *simpliciter* to the Holy See—depending on the dignity of the ecclesiastical person offended—is now incurred only by those who venture *(ausus fuerit)* to cite a dignitary of the Church before a secular tribunal without having first obtained permission from the Holy See. With regard to the citation, without proper permission, of clerics and others below the ranks mentioned explicitly in canon 2341, the penalty depends upon the ecclesiasical status of the guilty party. A cleric who would venture to cite before a lay court another person who enjoys the privilege of the forum without having first obtained proper authorization from the local ordinary of the defendant, incurs *ipso facto* suspension *ab officio* reserved to the ordinary; a lay person guilty of the same delict is to be punished by his own ordinary with congrous penalties according to the gravity of his fault.—canon 2341.

[42] Canon 25.

[43] Cc. 8-9, X, *de consuetudine*, I, 4.

against either the natural law or the divine positive law; only a reasonable centenary or immemorial custom can nullify an ecclesiastical law which contains a *clausula* that prohibits future customs; and against an ecclesiastical law that lacks such a prohibition, a custom may obtain only if it is reasonable and in force for forty continuous and complete years.[44] A custom that is expressly reprobated in the law is not reasonable.[45] It is not an easy matter in practice to determine which of the clerical privileges are native rights and consequently of the natural and divine positive law, and which are strictly immunities that accrue to the clergy by ecclesiastical law. Certainly the clergy are exempt by divine law from those obligations and duties which are absolutely repugnant to the dignity and freedom of the sacred ministry; against these no contrary custom can prevail. The exemption of bishops and priests from military service in the strict sense of their obligation to bear arms in time of war seems to fit into this category.[46] The strong language employed in the papal letters which condemn the compulsory military service of the clergy, religious and seminarians,[47] as well as the severe sanction which the law attaches to the voluntary enlistment of a cleric without the license of his ordinary,[48] tends to support this view. However, as Coronata observes, inasmuch as not all authors agree that this is of divine law, the Supreme Pontiff, in extraordinary circumstances and if the public good absolutely demands, can dispense.[49]

[44] Canon 27, § 1.

[45] Canon 27, § 2.

[46] Cappello, *Summa iuris publici ecclesiastici,* pp. 468-470; Coronata, *Ius publicum ecclesiasticum,* 216-219; Vermeersch-Creusen, *Epitome iuris canonici,* I, 215.

[47] E.g., Letter of Pius IX to the Archbishop of Monreale: "iniquissiamam esse legem," "infandam perniciosam legem," "nefarium facinus quod perpetrandum proponitur adversus personalem cleri immunitatem," —Roskovàny, *Monumenta Catholica,* nn. 2367-2368; S. C. de Religiosis decr. *"Inter reliquas,"* 1 ian. 1911—*Fontes,* 4408; S. C. Consist., decr. *"Redeuntibus,"* 25 oct. 1918: "lex infausta," "grave vulnus ecclesiasticae disciplinae,"—*AAS* X (1918), 481.

[48] Canon 141, § 2.

[49] *Ius publicum ecclesiasticum,* p. 216.

The services of bishops and priests as military chaplains, and the employment of minor clerics in the hospital corps, as provided for in the concordats, is not to be construed as military service in the strict sense. Although the employment of clerics and religious in the hospital corps implies some deordination, it is not *per se* opposed to the clerical state, and hence is in no way contrary to divine law. Moreover, not each and every public office is absolutely incompatible with the clerical state; accordingly these can be and sometimes are permitted to clerics. The immunity of the clergy, however, rests in the fact that they cannot be forced by the State to undertake these obligations.[50]

But the bulk of the discussion regarding custom and clerical immunity has centered around the privileged forum of the clergy. Although the law of the decretals expressly reprobated the force of custom against clerical immunity, especially in regard to criminal cases,[51] and was extended to other violations of immunity in the annual publication of the Bull *in Coena Domini,* in practice the systematic violation of immunity by secular governments continued.[52] Nevertheless, as long as these prescriptions remained in force (at least in those places where the Bull *in Coena Domini* could be published) all privileges and customs contrary to clerical immunity were expressly reprobated.[53]

Suarez observed that in the decretals the reprobation of custom against clerical immunity was by no means confined to the privilege of the forum, but that the tenor both of the law of Frederick II and of Pope Honorius III clearly extended to any

[50] Cappello, *Summa iuris publici ecclesiastici,* p. 472.

[51] "Clericus de omni crimine coram iudice ecclesiastico debet conveniri, nec valet consuetudo contraria."—c. 8, X, *de iudiciis,* 1, 2.

[52] D. Govarts, *Certamen immunitatis,* p. 14.

[53] "Non obstantibus privilegiis, indultis, indulgentiis . . . necnon consuetudinibus etiam immemorabilibus, ac praescriptionibus quantumcumque longissimis aliisque quibuslibet observantiis, scriptis vel non scriptis, per quae contra hos nostros processus, ac sententias . . . quae omnia, quoad hoc eorum omnium tenores, ac si ad verbum nihil penitus omisso, inferentur, praesentibus pro expressis habentes, paenitus tollimus, et omnino revocamus caeterisque contrariis quibuscumque."—*Bulla in Coena Domini,* in Fatolillus, *Theatrum immunitatis et libertatis ecclesiasticae,* p. 404.

custom contrary to the liberty of the Church.[54] Suarez held that clerical exemption is simply of divine law, against which no human custom can prevail;[55] nor in his estimation could there even be conceived a case in which the silence of the Holy See in order to avoid greater evils might be construed as tacit consent to any such custom which would be in itself unreasonble,[56] and even partial derogation by custom was reprobated in view of the firm stand taken by the Holy See in the Bull *in Coena Domini.*[57] Reiffenstuel, who shared the view of Suarez that clerical immunity is more probably of divine law, arrived at the same conclusion, namely, that any custom contrary to clerical immunity is unreasonable on the ground that it is contrary to the liberty of

[54] "Licet videtur sermo [c. 8, X, *de iudiciis*, I, 2] esse tantum de privilegio Fori in criminalibus, nihilominus ab omnibus de tota immunitate ecclesiastica intelligitur, tum quia ratio textus in quacumque materia hujus exemptionis aeque procedit, tum etiam quia alii canones absolute de libertate ecclesiastica loquuntur."—*Opera omnia,* ed. a Carolo Berton (26 vols., Parisiis: apud Ludovicum Vivés, 1856-1861), tom. XXV (1859), lib. IV, cap. XXXII, n. 3. Hereafter this work will be referred to as *De immunitate ecclesiastica.*

[55] "Respondeo exemptionem clericorum nulla consuetudine amitti vel diminui posse. . . . Ratio autem hujus assertionis imprimis reddi potest ex illo fundamento, quod haec exemptio est de jure divino, contra quod non potest consuetudo praevalere."—*Ibid.,* n. 4.

[56] "Addimus vero, licet fingatur casus in quo, ad vitanda majora mala, hoce possit Pontifex in aliqua provincia permittere, nihilominus numquam posse per solam consuetudinem id fieri, quia talis consuetudo de se valde irrationabilis est, et multum derogans juri divino, et numquam potest praesumi tacitam voluntatem Pontificis illi assistere."—*Ibid.,* n. 8.

[57] "Etiam quoad partem per consuetudinem haec immunitas abrogari nequit. . . . Quoties autem lex non solum prohibet actum, sed etiam abrogat consuetudinem, non potest per consuetudinem derogari, quia lex ipsa praevenit et vires abstulit consuetudini ad derogandum se; alias esset inutilis illa clausula."—*Ibid.,* n. 9; "Certissimum est numquam intervenire in hac materia tacitum consensum Apostolicae Sedis, cujus auctoritate talis consuetudo jure communi prohibita est. Assumptum probatur, quia semper Apostolica Sedes per sententias, vel per expressa edicta his consuetudinibus contra libertatem ecclesiasticam resistit, et specialiter in Bulla Coenae singulis annis eas revocat, vel potius irritas declarat; ergo numquam potest praesumi tacitus consensus Pontificis."—*Ibid.,* n. 11

the Church.[58] Schmalzgrueber, who held a milder opinion than Suarez and Reiffenstuel with regard to the juridical nature of clerical immunity, nevertheless agreed that clerical immunity could not be abrogated by custom. Such custom would be unreasonable and in view of the then current ecclesiastical legislation could not be conceived to enjoy the tacit consent of the Holy See.[59] In view of the tenor of the express reprobation of customs contrary to clerical immunity, it is not difficult to understand how, even apart from their view of its juridical nature, the decretalists generally regarded such customs as unreasonable. Even as late as the last century De Angelis (†1881) upheld this interpretation.[60]

Nevertheless, as early as 1753, Pichler, who held that clerical immunity is "more probably immediately of divine law," arrived at the opposite conclusion. He noted that it was the opinion of many writers, whose view he shared, that, provided a custom can be proved actually to exist, it was not necessarially a *corruptela legis.* Pichler argued that such custom, although contrary to ecclesiastical immunity and condemned so frequently in canon law, nevertheless could be founded in the tacit consent of the pope and consequently could be legitimate.[61] It is to be noted that Pichler confined his observations on the force of custom in this matter to *causae reales,* and excluded from the scope of this view criminal cases of clerics. He pointed out in support of his contention that not every custom contrary to clerical immunity is a *corruptela legis,* that for instance the custom of pressing a counter-

[58] Reiflenstuel, lib. II, tit. II, nn. 240-241; lib. III, pars III tit. XLIX, n. 56.

[59] Schmalzgrueber, lib. II, tit. II, n. 99; lib. III, tit. XLIX, n. 58.

[60] De Angelis, lib. III, tit. XLIX, n. 2.

[61] "Certe non videtur credibile, quod Pontifex omnes illos Principes et Magistratus in quorum territoriis non ignorat vigere talem consuetudinem, alias de Ecclesia praeclare meritos velit vinculo excommunicationis esse innodatos, tamquam violatores Immunitatis Ecclesiasticae, urgendo suas leges circa hunc casum particularem, quarum observantiam propter invalescentem nimis usum contrarium, longissimo et immemoriali tempore continuatum, moraliter vix sperare posset."—lib. II, tit. II, n. 10.

claim against a cleric before a lay judge could be considered contrary to ecclesiastical liberty, but that none the less it is reprobated by no Catholic author.

That clerical immunity is formally of ecclesiastical law, although its reasons are grounded in divine law, and that it pertains to the honor and dignity of the Church, although it is not absolutely necessary for the conservation of the Church and can be derogated with the consent of the Holy See, are pointed out by Santi (†1885),[62] Wernz, (†1914),[63] and authors generally, in view of the practice of the Holy See in granting privileges derogatory to clerical immunity to civil rulers by tacit acquiescence to the actual curtailment of clerical immunity by civil rulers. Nevertheless many authors considered it necessary to regard these derogations as a species of delegation to the lay power by the Holy See. This is the explanation of Santi [64] and De Angelis.[65] Cavagnis, however, clearly points out that clerical immunity is not of divine law to the extent that clerics and ecclesiastical goods could not be subjected to lay jurisdiction without the delegation of the Church; for this is not the spirit of the Church, nor is it the intention of the State to proceed against clerics as if it were delegated by the Church.[66]

[62] Santi, lib. II, tit. II, nn. 27-29.

[63] *Ius decretalium,* III, 46.

[64] "At ob urgentes circumstantias, ob specialem conditionem locorum et temporum, potest Romanus Pontifex tolerare, vel etiam permittere, ut causae clericorum a laicis personis quibusdam in locis et certis sub conditionibus, cognoscantur et definiantur. Quae permissio si de christianis personis sermo sit considerari etiam potest ceu species delegationis ecclesiasticae, quae ex privilegio Pontificis etiam a laicis potest exerceri."—lib. II, tit. II, n. 30.

[65] Lib. III, tit. XLIX, n. 5.

[66] "Neque dici potest id tantum esse iuris divini, nempe sine delegatione Ecclesiae non posse clericos et res sacras subiici iurisdictioni laici; Ecclesiam autem per concordata et tacitam acquiescentiam hanc concedere permissionem. Siquidem hic non videtur esse spiritus Ecclesiae quasi si auctoritatem tribuat laicae potestati procedendi nomine Ecclesiae, sed tantum non vindicandi sibi iustum privilegium: nec laica potestas cum haec sibi impetrat intendit procedere ex delegatione Ecclesiae ipsius."—*Institutiones iuris publici ecclesiastici,* II, 182.

In 1889, Wernz pointed out that the immunity of the clerical forum could be derogated by custom, if the same were reasonable and legitimately in possession; that although its effect be less perfect or less favorable to the Church, it could not be considered a *corruptela legis* on that score alone; and that it could not be considered unreasonable because it could be based on the same motives that the pope recognized as legitimate when he expressly abrogated the clerical forum in many places; and was not therefore without the tacit consent of the Holy See.[67] The contrary view, however, was maintained by the Rota in a particular case in Italy, in 1910, which held that customs contrary to the privileged forum of the clergy must be reprobated as opposed to ecclesiastical liberty.[68] The publication of the *motu proprio "Quantavis diligentia,"* [69] was the occasion of much adverse comment from the liberals. These were answered in Germany by Dr. Franz Heiner (†1919), who had been an auditor of the Rota

[67] "Consuetudo cum vi juris divini abrogandi prorsus destituatur, forum privilegiatum R. Pontificis nullo umquam tempore auferre valet, at immunitas inferiorum clericorum, quo ambitu expressa Rom. Pontificis concessione in multis regionibus immutata vel quoad substantiam abrogata est, eadem etiam longaeva consuetudine in aliis regionibus immutari vel tolli potest. Quod enim temporum ratione habita R. Pontifex non paucis regionibus concessit, profecto nequit esse praxis irrationabilis, licet sit minus perfecta et favorabilis Ecclesiae; at etiam in aliis regionibus, eadem possunt vigere circumstantiae, ergo rationabilitas sive prima legitimae consuetudinis conditio non deest. Qua conditione posita, multo facilius habetur altera, quod consuetudo debet esse legitime praescripta."—*Praelectiones de iudiciis civilibus* (Romae, 1889), p. 260, as quoted by Heiner, "Das Motuproprio *'Quantavis diligentia'* Pius' X von 9 Oktober 1911 und der deutsche 'Rechtsstaat,' "—*AKKR*, XCII (1912), 274. This is repeated in Wernz-Vidal, *Ius canonicum ad codicis normam exactum* (vol. VI, Romae: apud aedes Universitatis Gregorianae, 1927), p. 48, n. (85).

[68] "Hoc privilegium Clericis *verius* competit iure humano consentaneo iuri divino; eorum enim immunitas a foro saeculari immediate quidem iure humano positivo est constituta; sed in iure divino fundamentum habet et intentionem . . . neque contrariam consuetudinem posse introduci, ea enim reprobanda esset, veluti corruptela iuris, utpote adversa Ecclesiasticae libertati."—*Causa Bagliani-Boni,* 15 maii 1910, *AAS,* II (1910), 495.

[69] *Fontes,* n. 694; cf. *supra,* p. 41.

since 1908,[70] and in the United States by Dr. Ayrinhac.[71] Both of these writers agreed that the provisions of the ***motu proprio*** did not apply to their respective countries by reason of long-standing contrary custom. Heiner's conclusions were questioned by Vermeersch († 1936) [72] but were confirmed by Cardinal Merry del Val, the Papal Secretary of State.[73]

Maroto (†1937) observes that the more probable opinion ***even after the motu proprio of Pius X*** admits the force of contrary custom in this matter.[74] Heiner called attention to the fact that he had discussed his view with several prominent canonists and with members of the Rota, all of whom shared his opinion, which had been given confirmation by the Cardinal Secretary of State.[75] Ayrinhac (†1931) pointed out that legislative customs may be established against this form of immunity; [76] and this view is supported by canonists of great

[70] "Das Motuproprio *'Quantavis diligentia'* Pius' X von 9 Oktober 1911 und der deutsches 'Rechtsstaat'," *AKKR,* XCII (1912), 270-295.

[71] "Clerics and secular tribunals," *AER,* XLVI (1911), 175-179; "The motuproprio "*Quantavis diligentia, AER,* XLVII (1912), 303-315; "Clerics before the civil tribunal," *AER,* XLVII (1912), 357-359.

[72] *Periodica,* VI (1912), 106-109.

[73] *Periodica,* VI (1912), 190.

[74] "Opinio probalilior etiam post Motum proprium Pii X *Quantavis diligentia* admittebat vim consuetudinis contrariae huiusmodi privilegiis saltem quod eas determinationes, quae iuris ecclesiastici merito considerari possunt, et dummodo salva sit substantia horum privilegiorum quae ad ius divinum pertinere videntur. Respectivi novi iuris idem tenendum est, at consuetudo debet normis accommodari."—*Institutiones iuris canonici* (Vol. I, 3. ed., 1921, Romae: apud custodiam librariam Pontificii Instituti utriusque iuris), p. 600.

[75] *AKKR,* XCII (1912), 270 and 280.

[76] May a well established custom be considered as equivalent to a general permission? Can there be a legitimate custom against the law of ecclesiastical immunity? Many good canonists deny it. . . . It has been officially declared that the Motu Proprio does not affect Germany for the express reason that there exists in that country a custom to the contrary, and so it is safe to conclude that legislative customs may be established against the privilegium fori and that their validity may be demonstrated with sufficient certainty, and that wherever they do exist they are not abolished by the Motu Proprio."—"The Motuproprio Quantavis diligentia," *AER,* XLVII (1912), 311.

authority.[77] Moreover, it is to be observed that the present law contains no clause which would reprobate a contrary custom against clerical immunity.

It is to be understood, however, that the distinction between the actual immunity enjoyed by clerics [78] and the right of the Church by divine law to establish their immunity [79] must be observed. The failure to observe this distinction has resulted in the confusion of the concept by the regalists [80] against whom Catholic writers have been constrained to express the fact that immunity (in the broad sense of the term which includes the right of the Church to establish immunity) is simply of divine law. Custom can never derogate the right of the Church over immunity; custom can never derogate any native right, even though the native rights can be called immunities in the broad sense of any exemption. But a well established custom against the actual immunity which clerics enjoy is a derogation against ecclesiastical law and not against a divine precept. This is admitted by many excellent authors; accordingly the canonical provisions regarding custom may be applied to immunity in the strict sense as distinguished from native rights and from the power of the Church by divine law over clerical immunities; against these latter no custom may prevail. Granted that tacit toleration of customs derogatory to clerical immunity in order to avoid greater evils does *not necessarily* and in all cases amount to tacit consent,[81] neverthless *in some cases* it may amount to

[77] Blat, *Commentarium textus codicis iuris canonici*, lib. II, n. 56; Cocchi, *Commentarium in codicem iuris canonici*, t. II, n. 36; Toso, *In codicem iuris canonici commentaria minora*, ad c. 120; Chelodi, *Ius de personis*, p. 194, n. 6; Cappello, *Summa iuris publici ecclesiastici*, pp. 446-447; *Coronata, Ius publicum ecclesiasticum*, p. 195; Ottaviani, *Institutiones iuris publici ecclesiastici*, I, 391; Augustine, *A commentary on the new code of canon law*, II (6. ed., St. Louis: B. Herder Book Co., 1936), 64.

[78] As applied in canons 120, § 1, and 122.

[79] As exemplified in canon 1553, § 1, 3°.

[80] The opinion of the regalists will be discussed in the next chapter.

[81] The excommunication promulgated in *AAS*, XX (1928), 146, in the matter of a famous case in the United States is a case in point, and indicates that the view cannot be held that custom has completely abolished

such. Granted that the changed conditions of modern society no longer require *the complete exemption of the clergy and their goods from secular jurisdiction,* on the other hand, mere popular opinion or the whim of a civil ruler is insufficient to bring about a change unless there be at least the *tacit* consent of the Church. For the Church, and not the State, has competence over this question of fact. Insofar as it is necessary for the welfare of the Church, therefore, clerical immunity must be upheld. For a long time the Church tacitly tolerated, and now at least to some extent positively permits, derogations through privileges, concordats and even by custom—not of any precept of the natural or divine positive law, which would be absurd—of her own laws concerning clerical immunity.[82]

The discussion of the *historical origin* of clerical immunity has been somewhat detailed due to the fact that a review of all the salient facts is necessary in order to understand the positions of various schools regarding its *juridical origin* which will be discussed in the second part of this thesis.

the privileged forum. The precise reason for the excommunication is mentioned in the decree: the guilty parties *had neglected to obtain permission from the Holy See* to convene *their Ordinary* in a civil court.

[82] In his textbook, *De processu criminali ecclesiastico,* edited by Dr. A. Wynen (Romae, 1912), p. 3, Dr. Heiner does not sufficiently clarify the distinction between the proper and exclusive right of the Church which is the *basis of immunity,* and immunity properly so called. His list of matters which belong to the proper and exclusive competence of the Church must be corrected in the light of the provision of canon 1553, § 1, 3°. However, the very fact that this book was the work of two distinguished auditors of the Rota (it was composed by Heiner and translated into Latin and edited by Wynen) and was published with the *Imprimatur* of the Vicariate of Rome itself, together with the fact that the present law does not expressly reprobate custom against clerical immunity insofar as it is of ecclesiastical law, constitute sufficient evidence that the general conclusion which Heiner borrowed from Wernz (cf. *supra,* p. 48) is a valid one.

PART II
PUBLIC LAW INQUIRY

THE JURIDICAL ORIGIN OF CLERICAL IMMUNITY

Throughout the course of the legislation outlined in the preceding section of this work there runs a single current of thought: *Ecclesiastical Immunity exists by divine as well as by human law.* No explanation which denies or doubts this proposition can escape the note of heresy; for the opinion which asserts that there is no element of divine law whatever in this canonical institution has been specifically condemned in the Syllabus. This —the view of the regalists—must be sharply differentiated from the various views of orthodox theologians and canonists. It is disposed of in the first chapter of this section.[1]

The precise juridical problem of the right or title of clerical immunity is the theme of the last three chapters of this section. It is a discussion which for a long time divided theologians and canonists into two opposing schools.[2] In their extreme forms neither view is admissible; in their moderate forms they can easily be reconciled: one group asserted what the other did not deny. The evolution of a clearer terminology has succeeded in bringing about the proper alignment of what is correct in two apparently contradictory views of the same subject. The presentation of these views by way of comparison and contrast, the observation of the principal contributions of canonists and moralists towards the ultimate solution of the problem, and the evaluation of the now common doctrine[3] constitute the chief matters of concern in this section—the PUBLIC LAW INQUIRY into the JURIDICAL ORIGIN OF CLERICAL IMMUNITY.

[1] Chap. V.

[2] The old "opinion of the canonists"—that clerical immunity is formally of divine law—together with the arguments adduced in its favor are evaluated in Chap. VI; the view that was formerly called the opinion of the theologians"—that it is of ecclesiastical law—along with the arguments urged in its support are discussed in Chap. VII.

[3] The rise and development of the doctrine now common among ecclesiastical writers form the subject of Chap. VIII.

Chapter V

THE THEORY THAT ALL CLERICAL IMMUNITY IS BASED UPON CIVIL LAW

Directly opposed to the common doctrine of Catholic theologians and canonists that a basis for clerical immunity exists in divine natural and positive law and that the Church is exercising her native right in constituting exemptions of her clergy from civil jurisdiction insofar as such exemption is necessary or useful for the maintenance of the honor and reverence due to the clerical state, is the view taken commonly by Protestants, regalists of every sort and modern liberals, who contend that immunities are merely civil laws and proceed entirely from the good pleasure of the secular government in their origin, in their essence, and in their abrogation. This position is the logical outcome of the contention of the Protestants that the Church is subject to the State, or of the "caeseropapist" notion that the independence of the Church is so circumscribed in practice as to be rendered almost nugatory. This opinion is in manifest and direct contradiction to the Catholic doctrine of the juridcal perfection and independence of the Church. It rests upon a false interpretation of the facts regarding the history of clerical immunity, and contradicts the statements that have been seen above regarding the juridical origin of clerical immunity which must be held by all Catholics.[1]

The arguments urged in support of the view that clerical immunity is a mere concession of the civil authority were derived from Scripture,[2] from history, and from the principles that the Church has no right to interfere with the "manifest" rights of

[1] *Supra*, p. 3, note 11; cf. De Angelis, lib. II, pars II, tit. XLIX; Cappello, *Summa iuris publici ecclesiastici*, p. 456; Cavagnis, *Institutiones iuris publici ecclesiastici*, II, 183-185; Coronata, *Ius publicum ecclesiasticum*, p. 207; Ottaviani, *Institutiones iuris publici ecclesiastici*, I, 401.

[2] Catholic writers admit that no text in Sacred Scripture gives rise to a strict right of clerical immunity which could be construed as binding in justice. This is further developed in a succeeding chapter.

the civil government over its subjects and that members of a twofold society are bound to observe the laws of the State as well as those of the Church. The argument from history, in the main, consists in an over-accentuation of the *fact* that immunities were actually granted to the clergy at various times by beneficent kings. This argument, however, fails to admit conclusions from this fact which one cannot deny if he is to have a true picture of the development of clerical immunity. This position ignores the firm stand taken by popes and councils and soundly established in the law of the decretals [3] which it refuses to accept as binding in the matter. The basis of the argument that clergymen are members of the State in no way different from other citizens and that, accordingly, the Church is guilty of interference with the "manifest rights of princes" in insisting upon clerical exemption is, of course, a corollary of the priniciple of complete separation of Church and State. In support of their arguments Protestants, regalists and present-day liberals have urged the quototion: "Render therefore to Caesar the things that are Caesar's; and to God the things that are God's[4]. It must be said that these arguments were advanced with more vituperation than with a fair analysis of all the facts.

Article 1. The Forerunners of Protestantism

In the papal bull in which he condemned the errors of Marsilius of Padua and John of Jandun, Pope John XXII outlined the chief propositions of the authors of the *Defensor pacis;* namely, that Christ appointed no visible head of the Church but that the authority of the Pope was no different from that of the other priests and bishops, that Christ Himself was directly subject to the State in temporal matters, that the appointment and dismissal of the pope is the prerogative of the emperor, and that the entire Church is incapable of applying any coercive penalty unless delegated to do so by the emperor.[5] Such a system postu-

[3] Cf. *supra*, p. 30, for bird's-eye view of this.

[4] Matt. XXII, 21.

[5] Const. *"Licet iuxta"* 23 oct. 1327—*Fontes,* n. 38; cf. *supra*, p. 28.

lates the absolute dependence of the Church upon civil society. It denies all ecclesiastical jurisdiction of the external forum. It would take away the very right of the Church and of the clergy to any independence of the secular authority whatsoever; and, in consequence, it would make all enjoyment of clerical immunity fully dependent upon the good pleasure of the civil rulers.[6]

With these propositions as premises, it is easy to conclude what was the attitude of Marsilius towards the question of clerical immunity. He declared simply that every priest or bishop is and ought to be subject to the jurisdiction of the temporal ruler in the very same manner that lay persons are subject, and attempted to demonstrate his thesis by painting a picture of the disastrous effects of clerical exemption. Briefly, his argument was that the Christian religion deprives no one of his right: but if the pope or any other bishop were exempt from secular jurisdiction he could withdraw the clergy from their subjection to temporal rulers and subject them to himself as (he claimed) the popes, especially Boniface VIII, actually had done, apparently with the intention of increasing their temporal power;[7] whence it would necessarialy follow that the jurisdiction of secular princes would practically be annulled. The great fear of Marsilius was that the majority of mankind would become members of the clergy or of the religious orders, and so share in the clerical exemptions; consequently the authority of the civil prince would be fruitless inasmuch as he would be bereft of subjects and practically no one would remain to undertake the public burdens. Marsilius closed his argument with the observation that those who enjoy civil honors and public services, such as the peace and protection of the human legislator, should not be exempt from his jurisdiction, except insofar as determined by

[6] An excellent appreciation of the *Defensor pacis* and an analysis of the views of Marsilius towards the Papacy are contained in Hull, *Medieval theories of the papacy and other essays,* pp. 60-103.

[7] In fact, the action of Pope Boniface VIII to which the *Defensor pacis* refers (c. 1, *de clericis coniugatis,* III, 2, in VI°) was a restriction and not an extension of clerical immunity.

the civil authority.[8] These conclusions indicate a form of naturalism of the basest sort. They are but the logical deduction of a system which denies outright the sovereign power of the Church and would make her completely subject to the whim of the temporal power. They found an echo in the writings of all Protestants, regalists and modern liberals.

The opinions of the Waldenses, founded in Bohemia by Peter Waldo (c. 1170), and of Martin Luther (†1546) and Melanchton (†1561) in Germany, and John Wycliffe (a. 1375) in England, merit some consideration here insofar as they shed light upon their attitude towards the juridical origin of clerical immunity[9]

The view of the Waldenses in regard to clerical immunity found an echo several hundred years later in the teachings of John Hus (†1415) and Jerome of Prague (†1416), after their defection in 1408. Their notion may be dismissed with the observation that they spurned any idea of ecclesiastical privilege; for they denied the very right of the Church and the clergy to possess property, to have their own competent forum, or to be exempt from any obligations of citizens by reason of their sacred vocation.[10] Wycliffe held that a temporal lord could legitimately and meritoriously seize the temporal goods of the Church if in his judgment the Church failed in its duty, that indeed the temporal lord had a strict obligation to do so; moreover, that not even the supreme authority in the Church had the right to inflict punishment on any delinquent, cleric or lay, but that this

[8] *The Defensor Pacis of Marsilius of Padua*, edited by C. W. Previté-*Orton* (Cambridge, 1928), pp. 183-184.

[9] Their propositions, in the form in which they were condemned by the University of Paris, are summarized in a collection by Charles Du Plessis D'Argentere, *Collectio judiciorum de novis erroribus, qui ab initio duodecimi saeculi usque ad annum 1632 in ecclesia proscripti sunt et notati, auctore Carolo Du Plessis D'Argentere* (2 toms., Lutetiae Parisiorum, 1728). Hereafter this miscellany will be referred to as *Collectio Judiciorum.*

[10] "Item, privilegia ecclesiastica non curant, item, immunitatem Ecclesiae et personarum et rerum ecclesiasticarum spernunt."—*Collectio Judiciorum,* I, 93.

was the peculiar right of lay lords.[11] The similarity between these doctrines and the teaching of Marsilius of Padua is evident.

Article 2. The Views of the Early Protestants

The early Reformers—Luther (†1546), Melanchton (†1561), Vermigli (†1562)—and their followers expressed views on clerical immunity which were essentially a development and an application of those of Marsilius of Padua. They took for granted the absolute dependence of the Church upon the civil power and looked upon any claim to clerical immunity as sinful. Thus, in 1520, the Faculty of Theology of the University of Paris condemned as false, impious, schismatical, destructive of the liberty of the Church and tending towards tyrannical impiety, the proposition of Martin Luther that the princes may revoke ecclesiastical liberty and that clerics cannot resist such action without sin.[12] Likewise the University, on October 6, 1523, condemned the proposition, taken from the *Loci communes rerum theologicarum* of Philip Melanchton, that the divine law itself subjects priests in forensic matters to civil magistrates, kings and princes.[13]

John Calvin (†1564) considered the immunity of the clergy a mere usurpation of the natural right of kings, an institution which "has crept in through violence and fraud." His argument

[11] "Item, Domini temporales possunt legibus ac meritorie auferre bona fortunae ab ecclesia delinquente. Item, si Dominus temporalis noverit ecclesiam delinquentem, tenetur sub poena damnationis ejus, ab ea temporalia auferre. Item, quod nec papa nec aliquis praelatus ecclesiae deberet habere carceres ad puniendum delinquentem sed quilibet delinquens posset libere, quocunque vellet, transire, et facere quae sibi placeret."—*Collectio Judiciorum*, I, 96.

[12] *Index materiarum ex variis Lutheri libris excerptam per Theologiae Universitatis Parisiensis Facultatem:* tit. XVI, *de immunitate ecclesiasticorum:* Si imperator vel princeps revocent libertatem datam personis et rebus ecclesiasticorum, non potest eos resisti sine peccato et impietate. Haec propositio est falsa, impia, schismatica, libertatis Ecclesiasticae enervativa ac impietatis tyrannicae excitativa et nutritiva.—*Collectio Judiciorum*, I, 373.

[13] *IV. Propositio:* Ipsos sacerdotes, quo ad lites pertinet et judicia subjecit jus divinum magistratibus civilibus, Regibus et Principibus.—*Collectio Judiciorum*, I, 203.

was very brief, based upon his own interpretation of history, and was characterized by the omission of any facts which would indicate that the Roman emperors allowed the Church more than the cognizance of merely spiritual cases not already provided for according to civil law. Calvin's argument was more properly an assumption developed by some explanation rather than by positive proof, together with a conclusion which he took for granted.[14]

Pietro Martire Vermigli (†1562), a Florentine Protestant Reformer, attempted to refute the argument of St. Thomas that exemption of the clergy from the obligation of paying tax imposed by civil governments is in accordance with natural equity. Vermigli admitted that the exemptions mentioned in the Old Testament [15] had been given by princes who were moved by piety but not by equity. Vermigli taught that the lands of the priests mentioned in Genesis were immune from taxation not because of any particularly sacred character of the Mosaic clergy, but because these lands were worked at a loss and hence could not be taxed. In regard to the immunity from tribute accorded the levites by King Artaxerxes in I Esdras, Vermigli observed that this is not surprising inasmuch as the levites possessed no lands in Israel, but lived only by oblations and sacrifices. Similarly this author explained the immunity accorded to the priesthoods of pagan nations. He cited St. Thomas as in agreement with him that the exemption of the clergy from the payment of tributes is not formally of divine law. This may be admitted. However, Vermigli adduced the poverty of the clergy as the only basis in natural equity for the exemption, and attempted to refute the Angelic Doctor on that point. He observed that Christ did not make use of the privilege, but neglected to mention that Our Lord specifically declared Himself free from its obligation.[16] Regarding the argument from the words of Christ, it is to be noted that the context indicates that the point

[14] *Joannis Calvini institutionum christianae religionis libri quattor* ([ ] ed., Amstelodami, 1667), lib. IV, cap. XI, nn. 15-16.

[15] Genesis XLVII, 22; I Esdras VII, 23.

[16] Matt. XVII, 23.

in question was the payment of tribute to the temple, not to the civil power, as Coronata and Ottaviani observe.[17] Hence the use of this argument to support the contention originally made by Marsilius of Padua and continued by Protestants and Gallicans is based upon a false supposition.

Vermigli contended that all the strife over clerical exemption had been begun by Pope Boniface VIII, who "foolishly and proudly" (according to him) had asserted that neither by divine nor by human law have the laity any jurisdiction over the clergy.[18] He ascribed the claim to immunity to cupidity and avarice on the part of the clergy, and accused them of asking that they be not compelled to obey the magistrates who are their lawful superiors or to help the republic whose citizens they are. Although he could not see any reason why the clergy ought to be exempt from civil jurisdiction in any way, nevertheless Vermigli considered that it was within the province of the civil prince, at his discretion, to grant immunity to clerics who (in his own estimation) had seriously discharged their duty, as long as this was not harmful to others or to the clergy themselves.[19]

Together with Luther, Calvin, Melanchton and other Protestants, Vermigli considered that any attempt by the secular prince to release his subjects from the jurisdiction of his courts would be contrary to divine law. This opinion rests upon the assumption that the entire political power is vested in the State, of which the Church would be a part and to which she would be necessarily subject, without any proper competence of her own. Accordingly, it would be impossible to release one's subjects from the only jurisdiction which has competence over them—that of the State. This would be a violation by princes of their own innate right, regardless of any merely *de facto* privilege granted in this regard.[20]

[17] *Ius publicum ecclesiasticum,* p. 208; *Institutiones iuris publici ecclesiastici,* I, 403.

[18] C. 4, *de censibus, exactionibus et procurationibus,* III, 20 in VI°; cf. *supra,* p. 26.

[19] *Loci communes Petri Martyris Vermilii Florentini* ([ ] ed., Genevae, 1626), Classis IV, cap. II & XIII.

[20] *Loc. cit.,* cap. XIV.

In the eighteenth century, Justus Henning Böhmer (†1749), who composed a commentary on Protestant canon law according to the order of the decretals, considered any claim of an ecclesiastical forum independent of and superior to that of the secular court as "insipid philosophising from which Protestants abstain," argued logically that in Protestant countries all the clergy, including the Consistory itself, were subject to the authority of the prince, and that accordingly, for a just cause, ecclesiastical cases could be appealed to him just as any other cases.[21]

The chief criterion of jurisdiction in the Protestant system was territorial domination, to which everything in one's own domination was subject. The denial of the sovereignty of the Church and of her consequent right to exempt the clergy from civil jurisdiction followed from this premise. Consequently, in the Protestant system all clerical immunity is dependent upon the mere good favor of the secular prince, in its origin, its essence and its abrogation. That these principles are but the logical deduction from the view of Marsilius of Padua needs no proof. Their common denominator is *naturalism* which refuses to admit the juridical perfection of the power given by Christ to His Church.

Article 3. The Regalist View of Clerical Immunity

The principles which have just been observed had their counterpart within the Church, although in a somewhat less marked degree. Even men of such unquestioned piety as John Gerson (†1429), Bossuet (†1704) and Fénelon (†1715), who made eloquent protest of their devotion to the Holy See,[22] were none

[21] *Iusti Henningi Boehmeri ius ecclesiasticum protestanticum iuris canonici iuxta seriem decretalium ostendens* (5. ed., 5 toms. in 4, Halae Magdenburgiae, 1746), lib. II, tit. II, § XIII.

[22] For an excellent discussion of the views of these writers towards the power of the pope in secular affairs cf. Hull, *Medieval theories of the papacy and other essays*, pp. 106-114. Hull rightly concludes that "Bossuet has no theory to cover the real problem [an example of which is clerical immunity] of the necessary overlapping of the spiritual and temporal order. Peaceful cooperation is an excellent ideal: but it is no answer to the question as to the rights of the two powers."—p. 113.

the less the champions of the *Gallican Liberties* which aimed at rendering nugatory the exercise of ecclesiastical jurisdiction [23] by means of the *royal placet,*[24] the *appeal as from abuse,*[25] and other equally high-sounding formulas. Gallicanism had its repercussion in the attitude of the regalists towards their understanding of the juridical basis of clerical immunity.

The attitude of the "court cannonists" of the seventeenth and eighteenth centuries, as represented by Petrus de Marca (†1662) in France, Zegerus Van Espen (†1728) in Holland and Belgium, whose name had great weight in Germany as well, Joannes Nepomoucene Pehem (†1799) and others, differed from that of the Protestants in that it admitted the sovereignty of the Church. This attitude, however, posited in the Church only a *directive* and not an indirect power over the State in temporal matters. Hence, according to this view, various explanations were utilized in order to show that the law of the decretals regarding clerical immunity "was contrary to the manifest rights of kings" and must be considered inoperative in practice, or at least must be so construed as not to interfere with the jurisdiction of kings over their subjects, be they clerical or lay. All these explanations concur in ascribing clerical immunity in its origin, essence and abolition to the civil power. According to this system, the State can abolish clerical immunity without consulting the Holy See and even despite the opposition of the Holy See.

Petrus de Marca (†1662) quoted with approval the observation that had been made by Suarez (†1617),[26] namely, that the Holy

[23] The views of Bossuet and Pietro Giannone (†1748) in this matter were ably refuted by G. Antonio Bianchi di Lucca, *Della potesta, e della politia chiesa* (3 toms. Roma, 1745), lib. I, 116-190; lib. III, 496-582.

[24] "Potestas tamquam proprium civilis potestatis submittendi nonnulla acta religiosae potestatis, sive pontificiae sive episcopalis, inspectioni et adprobationi civili antequam promulgari et exequi valeant."—Ottaviani, *Institutiones,* II, 254.

[25] "Recursus ad auctoritatem civilem tamquam ab abusu auctoritatis ecclestiasticae, sive in causis iudicialiter dirimendis sive in provisionibus ordinis administrativae."—Ottaviani, *Institutiones,* II, 262.

[26] "Ideo dici privilegiata quia privilegio sedis apostolicae indultum est Regibus Francorum, ut ea delicta cognoscere possint."—*De immunitate ecclesiastica,* p. 523.

See had conceded privileges to the kings of France which were in effect derogatory to the privileged forum of the clergy. Regarding these privileges, however, De Marca remained studiously vague. Nor do Bellarmine (†1621) and Suarez throw much light upon their nature. Although Ferraris (†c. 1763) refers to privileges conceded to kings in this matter by Xystus IV (11 iun. 1474), Innocent VIII (1487), Alexander VI (20 iun. 1502), Paul III (10 oct. 1541) and Innocent IX (1591),[27] no trace of these grants can be found in the *Bullarium Romanum Taurinense*. The Holy Office in an instruction issued on August 3, 1639[28] had replied that royal privileges alleged to have been granted by the Holy See could not be urged as a pretext for according absolution in the case of reserved censures attached to the violation of clerical immunity in the bull in *Coena Domini*.[29]

De Marca concluded that the popes did not abolish the customs of the Gallican Church, even though they were somewhat contrary to the law of the decretals, but preferred to dissimulate rather than make innovations which would cause discord and offense. Nevertheless he suggested that it was more "in keeping with sincerity to consider certain crimes of clerics as *privileged* by royal law in some matters, and by the native right and duty of princes to protect and preserve their interests which cannot be restricted by even the Holy See itself," together with ancient and immemorial custom contrary to the decretal law,[30] even though this had been ruled out by the law of the decretals itself[31] and though even a centenary or immemorial custom against clerical immunity was considered unreasonable in the common estimation of theologians and canonists at that time.[32]

[27] *Prompta bibliotheca canonica iuridica moralis theologica nec non ascetica polemica rubricistica historica* ([ ] ed., 9 vols., Romae, 1885-1899), v. *Clericus,* art. II, n. 100.

[28] *Ad 2.—Fontes,* n. 726.

[29] Cf. *supra,* pp. 31-32.

[30] *Dissertationum de concordia sacerdotii et imperii seu de libertatibus ecclesiae gallicanae libri octo* (3. ed., Parisiis, 1704), lib. III, capp,. IX & X.

[31] C. 8, X, *de iudiciis,* II, 1; cf. *supra,* p. 44.

[32] Cf. *supra,* pp. 45-47.

An even more vehement spirit of liberalism is evident in the writings of de Lacombe (c. 1777), who made no pretence of an appeal to papal privileges, but submitted the thesis that the natural right of kings alone demands that all subjects—clerical and lay—be strictly bound by the laws of France and that whatever exemptions were accorded them existed only at the good pleasure of the king. In his estimation any custom contrary to the law of the State in favor of the clergy was due to pure condescension of royal favor and was in no sense a strict right of the clergy; the law of the decretals he declared to be without force inasmuch as it was contrary to the natural rights of the king.[33]

The same popular thesis of the regalists was propounded by Zegerus Van Espen (†1728), whose chief argument was that history shows that Gratian, depending upon the Pseudo-Isidorian Decretals, distorted the sense of the legislation of the early councils, and that canonists, especially Cardinal Bellarmine, in deference to the statements of Pope Boniface VIII and to the Council of Trent, had maintained an indiscreet zeal in declaring that clerical immunity was of divine law and in conceding to the pope the power to withdraw the clergy from the jurisdiction of temporal rulers. Van Espen's own observation was that clerical immunity in the last analysis must not be offensive to the authority of the secular prince and can exist only according to his good pleasure.[34]

It is in the section on criminal jurisdiction that Van Espen succinctly stated the thesis which later was condemned in explicit terms by the Holy See. Van Espen admitted that it was the law of the decretals and the common opinion of the decretalists in conformity with them that all criminal cases of clerics must be judged by the ecclesiastical tribunal. He insisted, however, that under no circumstances may the immunity of the clergy be harm-

[33] *Recueil de jurisprudence canonique et beneficiale par ordre alphabetique* (2. *ed. Paris,* 1771), *vv. delit commun, cas privilegié & privileges des ecclesiastiques.*

[34] *Jus ecclesiasticum universum* (5 toms. in 4, Lugduni et Lovanii, [ ] ed. 1753) tom. I, pars II, sect. IV, tit. IV-V.

ful to the authority of secular princes, from whose indult it flows. "Hence it evidently follows that the exemption of the clergy from lay jurisdiction even in criminal cases does not proceed from the natural or divine law, nor from ecclesiastical decrees, but only from the laws of emperors and princes," and despite the authority of the decretals was to be judged by these norms alone.[35]

The undiluted spirit of erastianism in its undue subservience to the State which, by consequence leads to the denial of the power of the *Magisterium* of the Church, is clearly delineated in Van Espen's plea not to heed the decrees of the Holy See on clerical immunity, but to maintain local customs and the edicts of civil rulers, upon whose mere volition he rested the basis of clerical immunity. That his thesis is contradicted by facts which he either fails to mention or misinterprets has been sufficiently discussed in the historical section of this treatise. His view was based upon a denial of the right of the Church herself to judge regarding the necessity or suitability of clerical immunity and of the fact that ecclesiastical laws designed to protect the Church may not be disturbed with impunity by the civil power. Needless to say, the view of Van Espen is at variance with the morally unanimous *consensus* of theologians and canonists.

In Austria, these same principles were outlined with equal clarity by John Joseph Nepomoucene Pehem (†1799), one of the principal ecclesiastical advisers of Franz Joseph II (1780-1790).[36] Pehem's thesis was simply that clerics in secular matters are *per se* subject to the secular forum, upon the testimony of the apostles, against which are opposed arguments on the grounds of the dignity of the priesthood, quotations from Sacred Scripture, the rescripts of the popes and the statutes of the councils. Whatever exemption clerics may enjoy in this matter, therefore, is unquestionably due entirely to the piety and beneficence of secular princes, and not to the decrees of the popes; that the civil prince can withdraw all temporal cases from ecclesiastical

[35] *Ibid.*, tom. II, pars III, tit. IIII, capp. I-II.

[36] This emperor is known to history as the "sacristy emperor" because of his officious interference in purely ecclesiastical affairs.

consistories; and that the clergy are *per se* obliged to undertake public burdens.[37]

The line of argumentation pursued by Pehem, Van Espen and the other regalists leaves no room for the indirect superiority of the Church over the State in temporal matters, even granting the higher purpose of the Church. Their position is based upon the assumption that the State admits of no higher power, even indirectly, which would prevail over it in case of a conflict of rights. The view is naturalistic and Erastian to the core, the logical consequence of the position of Marsilius of Padua, and in effect—at least in the matter of clerical immunity—not substantially different from the stand taken by Protestants. In the form proposed by these writers, the opinion is condemned by the Holy See. [38]

Article 4. The Liberalist View of Clerical Immunity

Those modern writers whose position is based upon a denial of the right of the Church to exempt her clergy from lay jurisdiction or from any of the common civil obligations of citizens on the ground that all rights emanate from the State, and, in consequence, deny the right of the Church to function as a perfect society, are grouped together under the various terms liberal, positivist, laicist, etc. [39] Liberalism, whether it be *extreme* in which case it involves an absolute denial of the proposition that the Church can exist and function as a perfect society, or *moderate* which admits the juridical personality of the Church but denies her any superiority over civil society, or finally so called *"Catholic" liberalism* which grants both the independence and the superiority of the Church but contends that practically her rights are not to be urged, especially with regard to the exercise of coercive power, relations with the State, insistence on immunities and the like, involves a theoretical and practical limitation of the proper

[37] *Praelectiones in jus ecclesiasticum universum* (Viennae, 1785), pars I, sect. II, cap. II, nn. § 709-726.

[38] Cf. *Syllabus errorum,* propp. 30, 31, 32—Denzinger, *Enchiridion Symbolorum,* nn. 1730, 1731, 1732.

[39] Cappello, *Summa iuris publici ecclesiastici,* pp. 178-180.

function of the Church. In its extreme form, liberalism is condemned in the Syllabus of Pope Pius IX.[40] Its concept of the Church as no different from any other society existing within the State was clearly indicated and vigorously refuted by Pope Leo XIII.[41]

The position of the liberals is essentially no different from that of their predecessors—the regalists. Their premises, their method of argumentation and their conclusions are the same. Their position is very well represented by Francesco de Paula G. Vigil, a Peruvian priest, whose book [42] was condemned by an apostolic letter of Pope Pius IX. [43] Shortly after this, Vigil composed a shorter edition of his work in which he attempted to answer the papal condemnation, reiterated his heretical doctrines, and expressed surprise that the Holy See would differ with his explanation of the facts of history and the nature of clerical immunity. [44] Vigil drew heavily upon Van Espen and other regalist writers for his sources and did little more than restate their arguments from the history of clerical immunity; and declared that the Church did not even possess the power to establish immunities, and that civil law can be the only source of clerical exemption.[45] Although his predecessors had attacked the power of the Church over ecclesiastical immunity because to them this power constituted an unwarranted interference with a monarchical form of government, Vigil attacked it from the standpoint of the representative form of government. He argued that the existence of concordats should not stand in the way of the revocation of the ecclesiastical forum for temporal cases of the

[40] "Reipublicae Status, utpote omnium fons et origio, iure quodam pollet nullis limitibus circumscripto."—Prop. 39—*Enchiridion Symbolorum*, *n.* 1739.

[41] Leo XIII, litt. encycl. "*Immortale Dei*," 1 nov. 1885—*Fontes*, n. 592.

[42] *Defensa de la autoridad de los obispos y de los gobernos contra las pretenciones de la curia romana*, 6 toms., Lima, 1848.

[43] Pius IX, litt. ap. "*Multiplices inter*," 10 iun. 1851—*Fontes*, n. 510.

[44] *Compendio de la defensa de la autoridad de los gobernos contra las pretenciones de la curia romana*, Lima, 1852.

[45] *Ibid.*, Disertacion 8, *de la immunidad de las personas y de las casas ecclesiasticas en los judicios, ó del fuero ecclesiastico*, pp. 178-190.

clergy, inasmuch as its revocation was a necessary consequence of a representative type of government which proclaimed the equality of all citizens before the law, and that this must be the only consideration of the legislative body.[46] The errors of Vigil were ably refuted by Juan de la Cruz Garcia.[47]

Vigil as well as the other liberals and the regalists persisted in ignoring the simple fact that the papal documents which were incorporated into the decretals, as well as the famous decree of the Council of Trent and the clear statement of the traditional concept of clerical immunity by Pius IX in the *Multiplices inter* and the *Syllabus* do not have to be interpreted according to the opinion of Suarez in the sense that clerical immunity is *formally* and *immediately* of divine law. The common teaching of the decretalists and other Catholic commentators has been that there is no strict precept either in the natural law or in Scripture which would posulate immunity in strictly temporal affairs as an absolute necessity. Likewise the regalists and liberals neglect the principle of *canonization* of civil laws by the Church and her promulgation of them as her own legislation. This is entirely in keeping with their principle of subordination of Church to State, or at the least, of their denial of the indirect power of the Church to withdraw the clergy from lay jurisdiction insofar as this is necessary or useful for her ultimate purpose. Their position consequently denies the very right of the Church to decree and protect clerical immunity by her proper authority and is but a logical conclusion from their premises. Yet this power of the Church is of divine law; it is the *basis* of immunity. The denial of this right cannot be reconciled with Catholic truth.

Article 5. Refutation of the "Civil Law Theory"

It is commonly admitted by Catholic writers today that immunities in the strict sense of the term, i.e. exemptions from civil jurisdiction and from certain obligations which the State

[46] *Op. cit.*, pp. 195-200.

[47] *La seudo-defensa que el senor Vigil hace de los gobiernos refutada por si miasma*, Lima, 1866.

commonly imposes upon its citizens, which the Church accords to ecclesiastics apart from their strictly sacred capacity, are not formally of divine law. It can be said that the arguments advanced by the regalists can be granted thus far. But the regalist position does not succeed in establishing that the State is the *only source* of clerical immunity; for its arguments are not sufficient to prove that the Church lacks a native independence of the State and, by reason of the superiority of her purpose, an indirect superiority in temporal matters insofar as these are necessary or useful to the attainment of that purpose. Certainly the Church may not interfere with the natural right of the civil power; but the natural rights of the civil power ought not to conflict with those of the higher perfect society. As Ottaviani observes, the things that are Caesar's cannot be rendered to him to the detriment of the things that are God's.[48] The subjection of ecclesiastics to their lawful civil superiors is to be made *saving the reverence due to sacred things* and within the limits which the higher law dictates. It is for the Church to determine the necessity or utility in particular cases. The question of clerical immunity is an illustration of these principles.

It must be pointed out that no Catholic writer denies that many immunities were originally given by civil governments. No Catholic writer denies that these concessions came about by a gradual process. No Catholic, however, can deny either that the Church has a right to establish and maintain immunities that were not granted by the civil government, that those immunities which had been granted by civil powers had become established by the Church in accepting them, or that immunities can be abolished without at least the tacit consent of the Church. The actual proofs of the thesis that the Church is a juridically perfect society and has an *indirect power* over the State in temporal matters are advanced in the standard handbooks of public ecclesiastical law.[49] These propositions were outlined by Pope Leo

[48] *Institutiones iuris publici ecclesiastici,* I, 402.

[49] Cavagnis, *Institutiones iuris publici ecclesiastici,* I, 129-144; 248-250; Liberatore, *Droit public de l'eglise, 7-27*; 312-315; Cappello, *Summa iuris publici ecclesiastici,* pp. 105-154; 271-315; Ottaviani, *Institutiones iuris*

XIII [50] and represent the certain and practically unanimous teaching of Catholic theologians and canonists.[51] The proof of this thesis is the refutation of the position taken by all those who deny her power over the immunities. The actual proofs of this proposition from Scripture, tradition and from the consideration of the nature and mission of the Church can be indicated in these pages only in brief outline; anything in the nature of an exhaustive development of the details of these proofs is properly within the scope of a text-book or monograph on these points.

That the Church is a *true society* is evident from the fact that she possesses the four qualities of a true society, namely, a multitude of members, a definite unity, an adequate end or purpose of existence, and apt means for the attainment of this end.[52] That she is a *juridical society by divine law,* i.e., one which possesses the *right* to impose with the consequent *obligation* upon her members to observe, a community of faith, means and rules tending towards a supernatural end, is proved from the fact that her Divine Founder conferred upon her these elements binding upon her members by strict obligation.[53] That she is *distinct from civil society* is evident from a consideration of her origin, purpose and the means she enjoys proportionate for the attainment of that purpose.[54] The State is of natural origin; the Church is of divine origin. The purpose of the former is the natural welfare of its citizens; that of the latter is their eternal salvation. The means proportionate to the maintenance of natural welfare cannot exceed the natural order; on the contrary, the Church has the right to employ any means which

publici ecclesiastici, I, 169-207; II, 137-151; Coronata, *Ius publicum ecclesiasticum,* pp. 50-69.

[50] Leo XIII, epist. encycl. *"Immortale Dei,"* 1 nov. 1885—Fontes, n. 592.

[51] Ottaviani, *Institutiones,* II, 147 and note 27.

[52] Cavagnis, *Institutiones,* I, 31; Liberatore, *Droit public de l' eglise,* 8-10; Cappello, *Summa,* 36 & 107; Ottaviani, *Institutiones,* I, 169-170; Coronata, *Ius publicum ecclesiasticum,* pp. 19 & 48.

[53] Matt. XVII, 17; XVIII, 18; XXVIII, 18-19; Mark XVI, 16; Luke, X, 16; John XX, 21.

[54] Cavagnis, *Institutiones,* I, 132; Liberatore, *Droit public de l'eglise,* p. 20.

are necessary or opportune for the sanctification of her members. Primarially these means are supernatural; nevertheless natural means, although only indirectly connected with the mission of the Church, can be employed as well. To this category belong the clerical immunities. The *degree* of their necessity or utility may vary; but they are within the competence of the Church; it is for her to determine both the necessity and its degree.

From these considerations it is evident that the Church is a *perfect society,* supreme in her proper sphere, universal and necessary.[55] These principles are denied by the Protestants and liberals; they are admitted by the regalists who, nevertheless, propose a system of strict coordination between Church and State but do not provide sufficiently for the case of a juridical conflict between the two perfect societies. Nor does the system advanced by some Catholic scholars which would admit an indirect superiority of the Church but limit it to matters *ratione peccati.* The only system that can adequately explain the right of the Church to remove the clergy from secular jurisdiction insofar as this is necessary or suitable is that which makes the basis of the indirect superiority of the Church *the consideration of her higher purpose.* This is the common teaching of writers in public ecclesiastical law. Cavagnis outlines these relations between the Catholic Church and the Catholic State (where alone the clerical immunities can be expected to flourish) in the following propositions:

I. In temporal matters, under their temporal aspect, the Church has no power over civil society;

II. In spiritual matters, civil society can exercise no power, these pertain exclusively to the Church;

[55] The proofs of this proposition from the Will of Christ, the testimony of tradition, the nature of the Church and the absurdity of the consequences which would follow if Christ had not sufficiently provided the Church with all the means necessary for the attainment of eternal beatitude are developed in Cavagnis, *Institutiones,* I, 133-188; Liberatore, *Droit public de l'eglise, pp.* 20-28; Cappello, *Summa,* 107-145; Ottaviani, *Institutiones,* I, 185-209; Coronata, *Ius publicum ecclesiasticum,* pp. 52-i9.

III. By reason of her higher ultimate purpose, the Church is juridically superior to civil society, the latter is consequently indirectly subordinate to the Church;

IV. In temporal matters that are necessary either *per se* or *per accidens* to the spiritual purpose of the Church, the Church exercises her proper authority, to which the State has an obligation to accede;

V. The authentic judgment in case of a conflict of rights between spiritual and temporal affairs, or a dispute concerning the necessity of temporal means for a spiritual end in a given case pertains to the Church.[56] These identical principles are outlined and proved also by Cappello,[57] Coronata,[58] Ottaviani,[59] and Catholic writers generally.

The exercise of ecclesiastical jurisdiction is a native right of the Church which flows directly from her nature as a juridically perfect society, as Coronata observes, and is the *basis or efficient cause* of clerical immunity.[60] This exercise of the Church's native right was impugned by the regalists and is ignored today by the liberals and considered a mere usurpation of the natural jurisdiction of temporal rulers. Accordingly, it has been necessary to outline, however briefly, the basis upon which immunity rests.

The question of fact regarding the effect of clerical immunity upon the rights of the State has never been easy to resolve. As can be expected, it has been greatly exaggerated by those whose major concern has been the defense of the rights of the State against what they are pleased to consider usurpations by the Church. The controversy regarding the effect of clerical immunity upon the welfare of the State cannot rightly be solved by the State alone, because it is a matter of conflict between secular and ecclesiastical jurisdiction, and has to be terminated according to the principles outlined above. The State is per-

[56] *Institutiones,* 244-253.

[57] *Summa,* 311-314.

[58] *Ius publicum ecclesiasticum,* pp. 108-116.

[59] *Institutiones,* I, 148-169.

[60] *Ius publicum ecclesiasticum, p.* 94 *and note* 1.

fectly within its rights if it informs the supreme ecclesiastical legislator of its grievances. On her part, the Church can expressly or tacitly restrict clerical immunity insofar as that is consistent with justice and necessity, either by making a change in her general law, by granting dispensations and special privileges, by allowing the curtailment of immunity by particular law such as a concordat, or by admitting derogation by custom. In fact, the Church has met new conditions that are adverse to a complete exemption of the clergy from secular jurisdiction in all these ways. But she has condemned any doctrine that would restrict or deny her right in the matter of the exemption of the clergy from secular authority.

Chapter VI

THE THEORY THAT ECCLESIASTICAL IMMUNITY IS FORMALLY OF DIVINE LAW

Throughout the history of clerical immunity a single current of Catholic thought can be discerned: immunities exist not only by reason of human law, but *in some way by divine law as well.* The precise extent of divine law in this matter has never been defined. In view of the common and true doctrine of Catholic writers today that *clerical immunity is basically, remotely and fundamentally of divine law,* but *immediately, proximately and remotely of human law,* there seems no need to expect any dogmatic definition on this point. But there was not always unanimous agreement regarding the precise part that divine law plays in the concept of clerical immunity. All the authors before the time of Schmalzgrueber (†1735) admit that this was a particularly vexing question. All agreed that with regard to strictly spiritual matters, the extent of the obligation of divine law presented no problem; they restricted the discussion to immunity properly so called, or the exemption of ecclesiastics in temporal matters from secular jurisdiction. Each recognized the solid probability of the contrary view; nevertheless a large number of writers—particularly among the canonists — insisted that clerical immunity in temporal matters could be proved from Scripture, from tradition and from the natural law to be simply an institution of the natural law. The opinion was carried to its apex by Suarez (†1617), who held that the privilege of clerical exemption (in temporal matters) is simply, immediately, absolutely and with all propriety of divine law. This view he diligently explained and defended.[1] Suarez carefully pointed out that he did not indicate as divine law that which was immediately instituted by the Church, even though the Church drew this power from a divine precept. He affirmed that clerical exemption from

[1] *De immunitate ecclesiastica,* pp. 395-397.

secular authority in all rigor is of divine law.[2] His principal argument was that God had committed the entire jurisdiction of the clergy, body and soul, to Peter and his successors, that the very nature of their work demanded their exemption from secular authority, and *confirmed* his opinion by testimony from Scripture, the common practice of all nations and tradition. This view he proposed as the most reasonable and most in conformity with the canonical texts which declared immunity to be of divine as well as of human law.[3] This opinion he carefully distinguished from the other views, and gave a separate treatment to the question: whether, apart from the immediate exemption of the clergy by divine law, their immunity could be introduced by canon law alone[4] or by civil law alone.[5]

Article 1. Presentation of This View.

The writers who lived before the time of the Protestant Reformation saw no need to make any distinction between those matters which are purely sacred and hence by their very nature exempt from secular authority, and those which are purely temporal cases of the clergy. Of particular interest are the two glosses which are found in the decree of Gratian. The first of these simply pointed out that the emperor, by virtue of his civil position, had no right to interfere in ecclesiastical matters or to judge the clergy.[6] Suarez observed that the glossator made no distinction here because none was necessary. The second comment of the glossator expressed this view with more clarity: before any constitution existed the clergy were simply exempt from secular jurisdiction, and all legislation which established the exclusive power of ecclesiastical superiors over the clergy were no more than declarations of [divine] law.[7]

2 *De immunitate ecclesiastica*, pp. 398-399.

3 *De immunitate ecclesiastica*, pp. 395-397.

4 *De immunitate ecclesiastica*, pp. 406-411

5 *De immunitate ecclesiastica*, pp. 412-421.

6 *Glossa* ad c. 5, D. XCI: Statuit Nicholaus, ut Imperator, qui tantum rebus humanis praesidet, se de rebus ecclesiasticis non intromittat nec de clericis iudicet.

7 Glossa ad v. *et discuti*, c. 11, D. XCVI: Ergo antequam esset aliqua

All the writers during the latter part of the sixteenth and throughout the seventeenth century testify that this was a knotty problem. St. Thomas Aquinas (†1274), who treated the question only in passing, as well as Hostiensis (†1271) and others were quoted by both sides as well as by the regalists, as partisans of their view. Yet, although both sides admitted the probability of the contrary opinion, neither would admit the conclusions of the other. It is interesting to observe the similarities between the two opinions; for, in fact, their similarity is more striking than their contrast. To canonists and theologians before the time of Bellarmine (†1621) and Lessius (†1623) the gulf between the two views seemed hopeless. Yet both sides made use of the same arguments; both sides admitted that the element of divine law must not be neglected. It was on the point of just how far there was an obligation in the natural law or in the Scriptures for the formal basis of immunity that they differed. Even later than 1621 there were many who neglected to accept the conclusions of Bellarmine and Lessius that the apparently contradictory views could be reconciled.

The main argument of those who held that clerical immunity existed formally by divine law was based upon their interpretation of the canonical practice in existence at the time of the decretals. The legislation itself amounted to a complete exemption of the clergy from lay jurisdiction.[8] Many authors were unable to understand how such a complete exemption existed, fortified with severe canonical penalties for its violation, if immunity were not of divine law. In their estimation, the wording of several important canonical texts which explicity referred to divine law[9] could not be sufficiently explained except by a literal application of them *to the civil as well as to the spiritual functions* of the clergy. The very essence of the clerical state,

constitutio, etiam clerici non erant de iurisdictione saeculari: unde omnes constitutiones quae emanaverunt, non sunt nisi iuris declaratio.

[8] C. 10, X, *de constitutionibus*, I, 2; c. 1, X, *de foro competente*, II, 2; cc. 4 & 7 X, *de immunitate ecclesiarum, coemiterii et rerum ad eas pertinentium.*

[9] *Supra*, pp. 3-4, note 11.

in their understanding, demanded its release from secular authority; the very nature of the Church, to their mind, connoted the sole source of jurisdiction over ecclesiastics. Towards the establishment of this thesis the arguments of this school were directed. It must be said that, in the main, these arguments were not designed to demonstrate a strict obligation in justice regarding ecclesiastical immunity in temporal matters; but an obligation of some sort was postulated by these writers, both from Sacred Scripture and from the natural law. The earlier writers show a tendency to be more strict in determining what to them was an obligation in the natural and divine positive law; the later ones were less inclined to base their conclusions on the intrinsic merits of the reasons advanced.

Although this was commonly referred to as "the opinion of the canonists" it drew many of its supporters from the ranks of the theologians as well. Chief among its supporters should be mentioned Joannes Dreido (†C.1540),[10] whose explanation, however, differs hardly at all from that of present-day writers. Dreido explained that although its *formal cause* was an irrevocable donation of princes, nevertheless it could rightly be called of divine law because it was so called in the words of canon law, because it was made after the examples of the Old Testiament, and because in spiritual and necessary temporal matters it is strictly of divine law.[11] The explanation of Joannes Dreido is quite similar to that of Hostiensis (Henricus de Segusio †1271)[12] whose opinion was quoted with approval by Cardinal Bellarmine.[13]

[10] *Joannis Dreidonis a Turnhout de libertate Christiana liber* (Lovanii, 1540) cap. IX.

[11] *Ibid.*, p. 109.

[12] *As recorded in Henrici Cardinalis Hostiensis suma aurea* (Lugduni, 1568), p. 282. Suarez observed (*de immunitate ecclesiastica*, p. 393) that in his commentary to c. 30, X, *de iureiurando*, II, 24, Hostiensis explained the words *"iure divino"* as the equivalent of "ecclesiastical law" in contrast with *"iure humano"* in the sense of civil law. This seems to be a perfectly satisfactory explanation of that particular text (cf. *supra*, p. 22). This explanation, however, is insufficient to explain all the texts regarding clerical immunity. Suarez rightly reprobates it (l. c.).

[13] Robertus Bellarminus, *Disputationum Roberti Bellarmini de Con-*

The point of departure of those who held this view was that ecclesiastical liberty (which would include the concept of clerics in their temporal as well as their spiritual offices) is so necessary for the conservation of the Church that it must be of divine law. A deordination against ecclesiastical liberty in the case of a single cleric, irrespective of his civil or ecclesiatical status is offensive to the whole Church. Inasmuch as this ecclesiastical liberty extends to ecclesiastic even apart from their strictly spiritual functions, it must be considered as of divine law. Such was the explanation of Philippus Decius Mediolanensis (†C.1576),[14] Navarrus (Martinus de Azpilcueta †1586),[15] Bozio Eugubino (†post 1600),[16] Azorius (†1603 or 1608),[17] Panormitanus (Abbas, Abbas Modernus, Abbas Siculus, Nicholas de Tudeschis †1445 or 1453),[18] and a rather long list of others cited by them.

Cardinal Bellarmine leaned towards this view, although his specific contribution was to conciliate the two opinions. To Bellar-

troversiis christiani fidei (lib. II, *de clericis,* [ ] ed., Venetiis, 1721), cap. XXVIII. Hereafter this work will be referred to as *de clericis.*

[14] *In decretalium commentaria necnon in tit. de privilegiis* (Lugduni, 1576), *comment.* in c. 10, lib. I, tit. II, nn. 12-18.

[15] "Quod clerici et monachi de iure divino sunt exempti a potestate laicali in causis criminalibus, et spiritualibus, et annexis eis ratione clericatus vel monachatus."—*Opera omnia in sex tomos distributos.* ([ ] ed., Venetiis, 1618) t. IV, relect. in cap. *Novit, de Iudiciis,* Notabile VI, n. 30.

[16] T. Bozio Eugubino, *De iure status sive de iure divino et naturali ecclesiasticae libertatis et potestatis* (Romae, 1600), lib. II, cap. XVII.

[17] I. Azorius Lorcitano, *Institutionum moralium pars prima* ([ ] ed., Brixiae, 1617), lib. V, cap. 12, q. 1.

[18] It is to be observed that both Panormitanus and Navarrus held this view only in regard to the privilege of the forum; both conceded that the exemption from secular tributes was of human law—*Nicolai Tudeschii Catinensis Siculi, Panormitani archiepiscopi vulgo abbatis Panormitani omnia quae extant commentaria in decretalium libros* (10 vols., Venetiis, 1588), *comment. in I decretalium,* tit. II, ad c. 6, de *maioritate et obedientia—Repertorium Antonii Corseti Siculi ad Nicoli abbatis Panormitani commentaria super decretalium et clementinam libros* (Venetiis, 1777), *v. clericus;* cf. *Martini ab Azpilcueta doctoris Navarri consilium sive responsonum libri quinque juxta ordinem decretalium dispositi* (3. ed., 2 toms., Romae, 1620), *comment.* ad c. 2, *de mairoritate et obedientia.*

mine is due the credit for a simplification of the terms of the argument and a clearer expression of the question.[19] Whether Bellarmine (†1621) influenced Lessius (†1623), who, although in a different camp, arrived at the same conclusion, would be difficult to say. Bellarmine's explanation of the conciliation of the two views is more detailed; it was intended to be a definite conciliation. That of Lessius, on the other hand, was a conclusion at which the latter arrived after a consideration of only one side—his own, namely, that no precept of divine law properly so called can be adduced for exemption in temporal matters—and a conclusion which he mentioned only in passing.[20] Neither school before the time of Lessius and Bellarmine seems to give evidence of having admitted the possibility of such a conciliation. Suarez (†1617) listed the view of Bellarmine as an explanation of how clerical immunity was of divine law, but attempted no conciliation with the contrary view, and made it clear that to his mind the theory which does not hold a strict precept of divine law was not the best explanation. For himself, although he admitted the probability of the other opinions, Suarez preferred to hold that a strict precept can be proved from the natural law and from divine positive law, and that an interpretation of the canonical expressions in the most literal sense was the most acceptable.

But the discussion did not end after the death of Bellarmine. The latter's view was simply consigned to the "divine law theory"

19 "Exemptio clericorum in rebus politicis tum quoad personas tum quoad bona introducta est *pariter jure humano et divino* . . . Nos per jus divinum non intelligere praeceptum Dei proprie dictum quod extet expresse in Sacris Scripturis, sed quod ab exemplis vel testimoniis testamenti veteris et novi per quamdam similitudinem deduci possi. Atque hisce fortasse conciliari poterunt Theologorum et juris peritorum sententias. Illi enim cum negant, exemptionem Clericorum esse juris divini, praeceptum divinum proprie dictum expresse in Scripturis exstare negant."—*De clericis,* lib. I, cap. XXVIII.

20 "Hoc modo videntur posse Canonistae cum Theologis reconciliari." —*De iustitia et iure libri quattor* (ed. 3., Antverpiae, 1612), lib. II, cap. XXXIII, dub. IV. For further discussion of this matter, cf. *infra,* pp. 99-100, note 10.

21 *De immunitate ecclesiastica,* pp. 393-401.

and once again the proponents of each side renewed their arguments. There can be noted, however, a greater shift on the part of the theologians into the opposite camp; henceforth there was less attempt to prove a strict precept from the natural law regarding clerical exemption in temporal matters. Each side began to give equal consideration to the arguments for the other, although the arguments themselves began to be presented in more concise form. Nevertheless, until after the time of Reiffenstuel (†1703) the view was regarded as the more common one. However, it can be observed that any real distinction between the two position was tending to disappear. Thus Diana (†1663), who assigns Molina (†1600), Lessius (†1623), Dominicus Soto (†1560) and Joannes Medina (†1580) to the opposite school, nevertheless employed the very same terminology as Lessius, admitted that there is no strict precept in this regard to be found in the natural law or Scripture, but strongly pointed out the influence of natural law *in dictating that the exemption be made.*[22] The position of Diana was no different from that of Joannes Dreido and of Bellarmine.

Other writers, such as Duardo (†c.1620),[23] P. Squillante (†after 1629),[24] Ambrosio (†c.1633),[25] Gonzalez-Tellez (†1649),[26]

[22] *R. P. D. Antonii Diana Panormitani clerici regularis resolutiones in tres partes distributae* (8. ed., Lugduni, 1635), pars I, tractatus II, resol. I.

[23] L. Duardo, *Commentaria in bullam S. D. N. D. Pauli papae V lectam in die coenae domini anno MDCXVIII in tres libros distincta,* lib. II, vers. 15, 2, 18, concl. 2, n. 16.

[24] *Tractatus de privilegiis clericorum* (3. ed., Neapoli, 1635), pp. 233, 283, 300.

[25] D. Ambrosio, *Commentaria in bullam Greg. XIV de immunitate et libertate ecclesiastica,* pp. 107-117.

[26] E. Gonzalez-Tellez, *Commentaria in singulos textus quinque librorum decretalium Gregorii IX* ([ ] ed., 5 toms., Venetiis, 1735), tom. II, *comment.* in c. 8, *de iudiciis,* I, II, n. 2. It is to be observed, *however, that this author* made the observation which does not seem to have been made by his predecessors, that the power of the Church to exempt the clergy from civil jurisdiction depends upon divine law. With regard to immunity itself, Gonzalez-Tellez held that it is of positive law. Accordingly his view will be discussed in the next chapter.

Paulus Laymann (†1674),[27] Prosper Fagnanus (†1678),[28] Joannes de Lugo (†1660),[29] not to mention many others, embraced this view wholeheartedly. All their opponents agreed to its probability and further attested its popularity. But to just what extent each author actually accepted the force of natural and divine law in the matter *as divine law and apart from its binding force as constituted by the Church* would be difficult to say. Engel (†1674), for example, entered into no argumentation but simply declared that the exemption was of divine law, without drawing any distinctions. His somewhat categorical presentation of the matter is interesting.[30]

A decided contribution towards the settlement of the controversy was made by Ernricus Pirhing (†1679), who suggested that the opposite opinion could be stated: *formally of human law, but originaliter et initiative of divine law.*[31] This expression, however, Pirhing rejected, not on its intrinsic merits, but because the view which attributed the exemption of the clergy immediately to divine law was then "the more common view of canonists, more in conformity with canon law, more favorable to the status of the clergy, based upon better foundations and rightly to be preferred." [32] Pirhing's own view was practically

[27] P. Laymann, *Theologiae moralis in quinque libros positae* (5 toms., Venetiis, 1719), lib. I, tract. IV, cap. 13.

[28] P. Fagnanus, *Commentarium in secundum librum decretalium Gregorii IX* (Venetiis, 1729), *comment.* in c. *nullus,* tit. II, nn. 1-67.

[29] *Disputationum de iustitia et iure tomus secundus* ([ ] ed., Lugduni, 1680), disp. XXXVI, sect. III, n. 100.

[30] "Exemptio clericorum est de jure divino. Exemptionem clericorum a jurisdictione laicorum nemo est qui ignorat, eamque *jure divino sit* ordinatam esse Pontifex et Patres (quorum utique est *de jure divino* cognoscere) aperte pronunciant, quos sequimur non curantes quae in contrarium asseruntur a Covarruv. et aliis DD. ibidem [allegatis]."— S. Engel, *Collegium universi juris canonici* (9. ed., Venetiis, 1760), lib. II, tit. II, § V, n. 38 & lib. III, tit. XLIX, § II, n. 23.

[31] Ernricus Pirhing, *Jus canonicum in V libros decretalium distributum* ([ ] ed., Dilingae, 1774), lib. II, tit. II, n. 107.

[32] "Concludo quod haec sententia sit communior Canonistarum, jurique canonico conformior; et status clericorum favorabilior, ac melioribus nitatur fundamentis, & merito praeferenda sit."—lib. II, tit. II, n. 112.

the same as that of Bellarmine. Moreover he noted that the theologians did not see a strict obligation from the natural law. He differed from Bellarmine, however, in this: Where Bellarmine tried to conciliate the two conflicting views, Pirhing contrasted them, and for the reason just outlined, embraced the stricter view.

Anacletus Reiffenstuel (†1703) quoted with approbation the conclusion of Pirhing in regard to this opinion. He flatly rejected the idea that ecclesiastical immunity and clerical exemption was only *originaliter* and *initiative* and not immediately and formally of divine law.[33] Reiffenstuel considered that, over and above the reasons adduced by Pirhing, the exemption of the clergy from the civil power in temporal matters was proved by the clearest texts of canon law; there was no reason why these should be taken in an improper sense. The contention that neither Sacred Scripture nor tradition could prove the existence of a divine precept, he simply denied, and was convinced that, taken collectively, these fonts do induce such a precept (although he does not say an obligation in justice). To his own satisfaction this was proved; but he admitted that it was not quite of divine faith and that there was opportunity for diversity of opinion on the point between theologians and canonists. Nevertheless, Reiffenstuel held that the opinion which he embraced was *very probable* and much more probable than the contrary.[34] But even in the time of Reiffenstuel, the controversy was far from ended, as he testified.[35] A later writer quoted several decisions which indicate that, at least during the early seventeenth century, the

[33] Nec pariter sufficit responsio aliorum, asserentium, quod Immunitas Ecclesiastica, atque exemptio Clericorum, dicatur esse de jure divino, non immediate ac formaliter, sed solum originaliter atque initiative: quatenus Legi naturali valde conformis est, atque a veteri Lege Divina fuit adumbrata."—A. Reiffenstuel, *Ius canonicum universum* (5 vols. in 7) Monachii, 1702), lib. II, tit. II, § IX, n. 213.

[34] Reiffenstuel, lib. II, tit. II, § IX, nn. 220-221; cf. lib. III, tit. XLIX, n. 235.

[35] "Celebris est haec controversia, atque in ejusdem resolutione plurimum variant Doctores, qui tamen generatim in duas extremas abeunt sententias."—lib. II, tit. II, § IX, n. 193.

view that clerical immunity is formally of divine law was held in favor at the Rota, and was by and large the more commonly accepted opinion.[36]

Article 2. The Arguments and Their Evaluation

The main arguments of those who held that clerical immunity existed formally by divine law were, naturally, based upon their interpretation of the canonical practice in existence under the law of the decretals. This legislation amounted to a complete exemption of the clergy from lay jurisdiction and from any obligation that could be imposed under a title of jurisdiction.[37] From the severe penalties attached to violations of clerical immunity in the Bull in *Coena Domini* [38] as well as from the canonical statements seen above,[40] all realized the vigor with which the Church guarded the immunity of her ministers; on the other hand they realized that the very basis of clerical immunity was denied outright by the Protestant sects. Accordingly, they made every effort to vindicate it. Granted that they did not necessarily admit a strict obligation in justice to observe clerical immunity from the natural law, they clearly believed that a divine precept was established nevertheless. Each author differed in his mode of presentation of the arguments; diversity can be noted in the degree of force each attributed to them. They are reducible to seven headings: to wit; 1. the general argument from the natural law; 2. the argument *a fortiori* from the Old Testament; 3. the argument from the New Testament; 4. the argument from constant tradition together with silence in regard to the beginning of this institution; 5. the argument from the statements of canon law. 6. the argument from the nature of the clerical state itself;

[36] Joannes Fatolillus, *Theatrum immunitatis et liberatatis ecclesiasticae tam theoretice quam practice excerptum juxta Gregorianam bullam* (2 toms., Romae, 1714), tom. I, pars IV, tract. IV, sectio I, n. 2.

[37] C. 10, X, *de constitutionibus,* I, 2; c. i, X, *de iudiciis,* II, I; c. 1-10, X, *de foro competenti* II, 2; c. 30, X, *de iureiurando,* II, 24; cc. 4 & 7, X, *de immunitate ecclesiarum, coemiterii et rerum ad eas pertinentium,* III, 49; cf. *supra,* pp. 22-24.

[39] Cf. *supra,* pp. 31-32.

[40] Synopsised on pp. 3-4, note 11.

and 7. the argument from the superior position of the clergy over the laity. A brief summary of these arguments, their conclusions, their answers to objections and an evaluation of what these arguments actually prove is in order.

§ 1. *The argument from the natural law.*

This argument can be summed up briefly as follows: among all nations the exemption of those especially dedicated to divine cult has always been recognized. This respect for the honor and dignity of the priestly state indicates a law of nature. Cardinal Bellarmine pointed out that theologians commonly distinguish three grades of the natural law; *first principles* which are immediately clear and evident to all; *proximate conclusions* that flow from these and are learned by an easy, evident and necessary consequence; and finally those conclusions which are deduced from the law of nature by a consequence that is not absolutely necessary nor entirely evident and which, accordingly, *need human constitution* in order to become effective. To this last category Bellarmine assigned the exemption of the clergy in temporal matters. This exemption, therefore, according to him, is stronger than mere positive civil or ecclesiastical law; it belongs to the natural law itself.[41] Other writers did not develop this explanation; they simply stated that clerical exemption was of the natural law. From the arguments on whose strength he depended to uphold his contention, Bellarmine did not venture to assert that there is any strict precept of the natural law which, without human constitution, would be of itself sufficient to demand that the exemption be made.

In criticism of the use of this argument to prove *from the natural law itself* any necessity of clerical exemption, it was demonstrated by the opponents of this view that it is not true that the sacred ministers of all nations have actually enjoyed full exemption from lay jurisdiction. Even if this were true, however, Cavagnis observes that the universal fact of clerical exemption would prove only the suitability of immunity; it also proves that

[41] *De clericis,* lib. I, cap. XXX.

there is some *foundation* in nature itself for this custom; it does not prove a strict inalienable right to such exemption from the natural law alone.[42]

Suarez argued that if such reverence was given to the clergy in the law of nature, *a fortiori* it belongs to the clerical state in the law of grace.[43] This is eminently fitting; it does not prove conclusively, however, that the dignity of the Christian priesthood itself is sufficient to exempt the clergy from all secular obligations and jurisdiction. From it there can be deduced a great indication of the suitability of clerical exemption according to the natural law *upon the hypothesis that such exemption is constituted by and derives its formal element from its constitution by positive law.* In the absence of such constitution it is difficult to admit that clerical exemption from all civil authority exists by virtue of a definite precept of the natural law.

§ 2. *The Argument from the Old Testament*

The argument from the Old Testament in support of this theory was employed in a twofold manner: *first* its passages were quoted along with those from the literature of the gentiles to demonstrate the argument mentioned above — that immunity is an institution of the natural law; *secondly,* it was employed to indicate the existence of a divine positive law. This it was admitted, established the immunity of the priests and levites of the Mosaic dispensation. What bearing would this have upon the law of the Gospels? Proponents of the theory answered this in either of two ways: Suarez answered that, inasmuch as the precept of immunity was a moral precept, it is still in force and was not revoked by the law of the Gospels, inasmuch as immunity is an institution so necessary for the welfare of the Church.[44] It may be conceded that this is sufficient to establish the immunity of the clergy in their strictly spiritual pursuits; with reference to secular affairs, however it is difficult to see how the precept still exists at the present time. Bellarmine admitted that no strict

[42] *Institutiones iuris publici ecclesiastici,* II, 181.
[43] *De immunitate ecclesiastica,* p. 391.
[44] *De immunitate ecclesiastica,* p. 401.

precept can be deduced from the Old Testament which would place clerical immunity proximately and immediately in the category of divine law; the indirect argument, *a fortiori* from the Old Testament, however, has great weight in establishing that clerical immunity is remotely, mediately and fundamentally of divine law without any precise obligation however, from the Old Testament itself. The observation made by him in this regard is just as true today as it was in his own time.[45]

The principal passages quoted in this matter were those which referred to the exemption of priests and levites from secular jurisdiction and from the payment of tribute in Egypt under Joseph and the pharaos;[46] the absolute exemption of persons and things devoted to the Lord by consecration;[47] and the exclusive jurisdiction of Aaron, the high-priest, over the priests and levites of Israel.[48] In the form presented by Bellarmine, this argument is acceptable; Bellarmine did not try to draw a strict right of clerical exemption from the Old Testament. It is true, as Schmalzgrueber indicates, that these texts can be used in support of a milder opinion.[49] Divine law can be considered an *exemplary cause of clerical immunity.* Later writers do not regard these passages as inducing any strict right of clerical immunity in the new dispensation.

§ 3 *The Argument from the New Testament*

From a text in the New Testament those who held that clerical immunity in temporal matters arose from divine law deduced an argument that the exemption of the clergy from tribute was a prerogative of divine law formally and immediately. Suarez, Bellarmine and other writers quoted the question of Our Lord

[45] Nos per jus divinum non intelligere praeceptum Dei proprie dictum, quod extat expresse in sacris litteris, sed quod ab exemplis vel testimoniis testamenti veteris vel novi per quamdam similitudinem deduci posse."—*De clericis,* lib. I, cap. XXXVIII.

[46] Genesis, XLVII, 22.

[47] Leviticus, XXVII, 28.

[48] Numbers, III, 10; I Esdras, VII, 24.

[49] Schmalzgrueber, lib. II, tit. II, n. 100.

to St. Peter and the response of the latter that the kings of the earth demand tribute not from the children of the kingdom but from others, and Our Lord's observation that the children are therefore free.[50] The argument concluded that inasmuch as the children are free, their goods are free as well. Clerics belong to the family of Christ, they are children of the kingdom, they have been removed from the authority of temporal superiors and transferred to the jurisdiction of their ecclesiastical superiors.[51] Suarez admitted that his interpretation was based upon an extension of the words: *Ergo liberi sunt filii.* This view read into the text a meaning and intention which Suarez and those who shared his view thought Our Lord had wanted to convey. Suarez admitted that the objection could be raised that such an extension was not contained in the text itself, and that no divine precept could be deduced from it. He answered in reply that, in all probability, Christ intended this extension of His words and that it is credible that He granted the privilege of exemption in the best possible manner.[52]

Nevertheless the argument is at best a private interpretation of the mind of Christ; even its best proponent admitted that our Lord gave no formal, direct and immediate proof of clerical exemption in temporal matters. Moreover, the passage in question refers in no way to any tribute to be paid to the temporal power, but to a tribute to be paid to the temple by virtue of the Law of Moses.

§ 4. *The Argument from the Constant Tradition of the Church.*

One of the strongest arguments adduced by Suarez to support his contention that clerical immunity is formally and immediately of divine law in the strictest sense, is the argument from the constant tradition of the Church, supported by the argument from silence in regard to the beginning of this canonical institution. This argument was quoted *verbatim* from Suarez, with appro-

50 Matt. XVII, 25.

51 Suarez, *de immunitate ecclesiastica,* p. 392; Bellarmine, *de clericis,* lib. I, cap. XXVIII.

52 *De immunitate ecclesiastica,* p. 392.

bation, by both Pope Benedict XIV (Prosper Lambertini) (1740-1758)[53] and by Cardinal Soglia (†1855)[54] The argument is as follows: when a tradition is constant and perpetual, it is an indication of divine law, especially when there does not appear any reason to attribute it to apostolic institution. The tradition of this exemption appears to be such; for it is so ancient that its beginning does not appear. Regardless of non-observance *in fact* by pagan emperors, the *right* of clerical immunity was not lacking. Ecclesiastical prelates always observed it insofar as they were able. This is proved by the ancient canons, which never refer it to apostolic origin, but venerate and observe it as divine law.

Suarez employed this argument as *corroborative proof* of his contention that clerical immunity is formally and immediately of divine law. It can be admitted that this argument proves that there is some basis for clerical immunity in accordance with divine law; it does not necessarially indicate that the exemption of clerics from temporal jurisdiction is formally of divine law. Cavagnis pointed out that the custom could arise from ecclesiastical law and from Christian piety. It was natural that, upon their conversion to the Faith, the emperors would extend to Christian clerics privileges that had been enjoyed by the pagan priesthood; it was natural, too, that the Church should enjoy them, lest she be considered less worthy of esteem in the eyes of the people.[55] The argument has full validity when restricted to strictly sacred functions of the clergy; it has great weight as an indication of the right of the Church to constitute clerical exemption. It proves, indeed, that the basis of clerical immunity is grounded in divine law, the agreement of this institution with divine law, but it is difficult to admit that it proves the existence of a divine precept against which all who failed to observe clerical immunity would sin on that score alone.

[53] *De synodo dioecesana libri* 13 *in* 2 *tomos* ([ ] ed., Venetiis, 1782), lib. IX, cap. 9, n. 8.

[54] *Institutiones iuris publici ecclesiastici* ([ ] ed., Parisiis, 1844), lib. III, cap. 1, n. § 58.

[55] *Institutiones iuris publici ecclesiastici,* II, 181.

§ 4. *The Argument from Certain Statements of Canon Law.*

The most convincing argument for those who held that clerical immunity is simply of divine law was their literal application of certain texts of canon law to the immunity of the clergy in temporal matters as well as in strictly sacred functions. The lay power simply had no jurisdiction over the clergy; the texts themselves did not distinguish, the canonists saw no need to distinguish.[56] These statements of popes and councils that violators of clerical immunity "have sinned against God and have not obeyed His commands;" [57] that "laypersons have attempted to usurp divine law when they exact the oath of homage from clerics, over whom they have no jurisdiction;" [58] that "ecclesiastical persons and their goods are exempt from the exactions of secular persons not only by human law, but by divine law as well;" [59] that "the laity have no power over churches or ecclesiastical persons;"[60] that "immunity is a very ancient thing, introduced by divine and human law;" [61] and finally that "immunity of the Church and of ecclesiastical persons is constituted by the ordinance of God and [fortified by] canonical sanctions;"[62] do not determine the extent of the obligation from divine law; they do not determine *in what way* the expression *divine law* is to be applied to matters of clerical immunity in the strict sense as distinguished from native right of the Church. It would not be quite fair to insist that each author who held this opinion considered that they implied a strict obligation in justice with regard

[56] Cf. Reiffenstuel, lib. II, tit. II, § IX, nn. 220-221; lib. III, tit. XLIX, n. 235; cf. also *supra*, p. 84.

[57] Alexander III (III Conc. Lateranen.), c. 19—Harduin, *Acta Conciliorum,* VI, pars II, 1681.

[58] Innocent III (in IV Conc. Lateranen, 1215), c. 14 = c. 30, X, *de iureiurando,* II, 24.

[59] Boniface VIII, c. 4, *de censibus, exactionibus et procuratoribus,* III, 20 in VI°.

[60] Innocent III (1199—c. 10, X, *de constitutionibus,* I, 2; Leo X (in V Conc. Lateranen, 1514)—*Fontes,* nn. 55-56.

[61] Council of Cologne (1266), cc. 7, 9, 11, 18—Harduin, *Acta Conciliorum,* VII, 565-566.

[62] Conc. Trid., Sess. XXV, *de ref.,* c. 20.

to temporal exemptions of the clergy apart from any human constitution. To Suarez and Reiffenstuel they implied a formal precept—a title of divine law in addition to human law. Bellarmine saw no difference between his own view and the opinion which denied a strict precept formally of divine law in itself. Other authors did not distinguish. Coronata expresses the view that is common today when he explains the phrases employed in these documents in the sense that they induce a mediate obligation from divine law, namely, through the medium of the authority of the Church. It is agreed by all that this somewhat restrictive sense is the better explanation of the above mentioned phrases and that the older canonists were inclined to deduce too much from them in their explanations of the juridical origin of clerical immunity.[63]

§ 5 *The Argument from the Nature of the Clerical State*

This argument was stated in its most succinct form by Prosper Fagnanus (†1678): "*Clerici res spirituales sunt, et ante omnem humanam legem constitutivam exempti a iurisdictione Imperatoris.*" [64] from the consideration of the peculiar sacred character of the clerical state—a total dedication of the person to God—many writers deduced the argument that members of that state were simply and absolutely removed from secular authority and placed under the sole jurisdiction of the ecclesiastical superior. Bellarmine presented this argument in vigorous terms;[65] Suarez gave it further clarification;[66] later writers copied it; and all were convinced of its effectiveness. In criticism, it was urged that the clergy do not cease to be citizens by reason of their total dedication to divine cult. If all civil obligations were incompatible with the sanctity of their state the argument would be fully effective. But such is not the case: there are many phases of life in which the Church never did withdraw the clergy from civil laws. In strictly spiritual matters, the argument has validity; in

[63] Coronata, *Ius publicum ecclesiasticum*, p. 210.

[64] Prosper Fagnanus, lib. II, tit. II, n. 2.

[65] *De clericis*, lib. I, cap. XXXIX.

[66] *De immunitate ecclesiastica*, p. 397.

others, there is no formal withdrawal of the clergy by divine law from the authority of the State. Only when there is question of conflct of rights does the Church *indirectly* maintain the exemption in civil matters.[67]

§ 6. *The Argument from the Exalted Position of the Clergy*

This argument differs only slightly from that considered in the preceeding section. The former can be considered the argument from the intrinsic nature of the clerical state; this can be viewed as the argument from the external relations of that state. Basically it was a repetition of a passage found in a letter of Pope Gregory VII to Herrimanus, Bishop of Metz.[68] It was presented by all the writers consulted. It is an argument from analogy: just as in the natural order the father should govern his children and the shepherd rule his flock, so in the supernatural order the cleric is both father and shepherd of his people. There is a great inconsistency in the spiritual father and shepherd being governed by members of his flock; subjection to its regulations and penalties would cause scandal and wonder to the faithful.

Granted the great inconsistency. In spiritual matters the priest exerts a great influence over his charges. His influence in temporal matters, however, is indirect; it can be exercised only by reason of a connection between the temporal and the spiritual and only because of the latter. He is not, therefore, in a perfectly analogous position with the shepherd and father. It does not follow that, by divine law, there is a formal and direct necessity for the exemption. It is entirely suitable. Its determination is vested in the ecclesiatical superior. Inconsistency does not give rise to strict necessity. Although inconsistent, the subjection of the clergy to the laity in strictly temporal matters cannot be proved to be intrinsically wrong or contrary to divine law.[69] It must be observed, however, that neither Suarez nor Bellarmine intended to imply that the inconsistency alluded to in

[67] Cavagnis, *Institutiones iuris publici ecclesiastici* II, 186.
[68] *MPL,* CXLVIII, 597 = c. 9, D. XCVI.
[69] Cavagnis, *Institutiones iuris publici ecclesiastici,* II, 183.

this argument indicated any intrinsic contradiction.[70] They employed the argument in its proper place as of a confirmatory character.

Article 3. Evaluation of This View

A detailed evaluation of this view would necessitate a repetition of much of what has already been said in criticism of the application of its arguments to all forms of clerical immunity. The view that clerical immunities are formally of divine law is given very brief treatment by authors today. Within its range there can be detected a great amount of variation by different authors. Suarez exemplifies one extreme; Bellarmine represents the other. The former made practically no distinction between immunities and native rights of the Church. He explained that immunity in temporal matters was a prerogative of the clergy, subordinated to the pope *in its manner* of operation and application; others saw it as the prerogative of the pope to apply and extend or restrict it (more properly a power residing in the pope to be communicated to the other clergy). Bellarmine showed that the two contrary views, at least in their more moderate form, were in a conflict that was more apparent than real. His dictum that "the canonists affirm what the theologians do not deny," cannot explain the position taken by Suarez; it did succeed in conciliating his own view with that taken by the more moderate proponents of the opposite school.

The main source of the diversity of conclusions seems to have come from a diversity of method. The method employed by those whose view has been outlined and criticised in this chapter was as follows: they first proved that in spiritual matters the exemption of the clergy is of divine law; then they extended their inquiry to temporal matters and concluded that these, too, had some basis of exemption in divine right. Not all of them implied that there was a strict obligation in justice in these latter affairs. In the main, however, they did not distinguish, as Bellarmine did, between those things that are *prescribed* by the divine law

[70] Suarez, *de immunitate ecclesiastica,* p. 400; Bellarmine, *de clericis,* lib. I, cap. XXIX.

and those which are *suggested* by it or simply in accordance with it. A further clarification of the issue can be observed in the "opinion of the theologians," whose view is considered in the next chapter.

Chapter VII.

THE THEORY THAT CLERICAL IMMUNITY IS OF ECCLESIASTICAL LAW.

The precise problem that had been debated between the two schools of thought within the Church regarding the juridical origin of clerical immunity was rendered more difficult than it should have been due to a lack of clear terminology and a diversity of approach to the question by the two schools. Not all of those who asserted that clerical immunity is of divine law postulated a *strict right* regarding the exemption of the clergy in matters temporal. To them, the term *divine law* did not necessarially indicate a precept in divine law immediately. Those whose view has been considered in the preceding chapter posed the question thus: Is the immunity from civil obligations and jurisdiction in temporal matters which clerics enjoy by civil and ecclesiastical law supported by arguments from the natural law and from Sacred Scripture as well? They arrived at an affirmative answer.

Some, such as Suarez, saw a strict precept; others seem to have evaded this question. On the other hand, many theologians in their treatises on justice and right discussed the question from a different angle. Their view was: Can there be proved to be an obligation in justice according to divine law itself to observe clerical immunity? These, together with some of the canonists, arrived at a negative conclusion. Both groups, however, admitted that the controversy was by no means settled by this discussion of it and that the contrary position was solidly probable. The theologians, together with those canonists who embraced their view, arrived at the conclusion that neither the natural law nor Sacred Scripture could solidly establish a strict right to clerical exemption in secular matters, and that consequently the formal cause of clerical immunity is human ecclesiastical law. Nor did they consider that this view contravened the statements of canon law, which they explained in the sense reprobated by Reiffenstuel and others.

Article 1. Presentation of the Question.

As has been observed, the canonists took as their point of departure the exemption of the clergy in spiritual matters and applied the same arguments to their immunity in secular matters as well. Their concept was more properly that of *ecclesiastical liberty* which includes immunities as well as native rights. More precisely, the theologians began with the concept of a single immunity—the exemption from tributes—and argued that this could not be construed as the object of a strict obligation directly from divine law. Their conclusions they applied to the other immunities as well. They agreed with those of the opposite school that clerical exemption in temporal matters is very much in conformity with the divine law, that it could be upheld by examples from the Scriptures, but they declined to see any strict obligation from the natural law alone. St. Thomas Aquinas (†1274) had mentioned the matter only in passing: he ascribed the immunity from tributes to the "privilege of princes" but observed that it was in accordance with natural equity.[1] Joannes Andrea (†1348) had simply observed that clerics inferior to the pope are subject to the king when they receive gifts from him.[2] Covarruvias (†1577) seems to have been one of the first among the canonists to assert that immunity in those matters that are not spiritual is simply not of divine law.[3]

[1] "Ab hoc tamen debito [sc. solvendi tributum] liberi sunt clerici ex privilegio principum; quod quidem aequitatem naturalem habet; unde etiam apud gentiles liberi erant a tributis illi qui vacabant rebus divinis . . . Hoc autem ideo aequum est, quia sicut reges sollicitudinem habent de bono publico in bonis temporalibus, ita ministri Dei in spiritualibus: et sic per hoc quod in spiritualibus ministrent, recompensant regi quod pro eorum pace laborant."—*Opera omnia* (34 vols., Parisiis: apud Ludovicum Vivès, 1871-1882), XX, *Commentarium in epist. ad Romanos,* 565.

[2] *Glossa* ad c. 2, X, *de maioritate et obedientia,* I, 33.

[3] "In rebus temporalibus, et in civilibus, quae spiritualia non attinent, Clerici et eorum res non sunt iure divino exempti a iurisdictione principum saecularium. Haec conclusio constat ex his quae tradidimus ad probationem posterioris opinonis contra communem: atque ideo, si iure divino absque humanis constitutionibus res esset examinanda, respondendum foret, in hisce temporalibus, nec clericos, nec eorum res a iurisdictione

Joannes Medina (†1546) propounded strong arugemnts against those who would impute the exemption from tributes to divine law. It is true that his arguments were quite similar to those employed by the regalists. Bellarmine particularly took issue with him on this point. True, Medina did not explicity affirm that the donation of kings was revocable; but Bellarmine observed that his arguments were open to a regalist or even a Protestant interpretation. However, it must be granted that Medina limited his discussion to a particular immunity—the exemption from civil taxes; his conclusion did not differ from that of St. Thomas. In his practical handbook he found fault with and controverted the view that this exemption is of divine law.[4] In view of his limitation of the topic, it would be unfair to accept at full value the criticism of Bellarmine. Medina was cited favoraby by theologians who followed him; he did not deny the power of the Church to establish clerical exemption, but proved that *no obligation* could be established in this matter by arguments from Scripture or from the natural law, and proposed the historical fact (not the necessity) of the actual exemption in the matter of tributes. His conclusion "non esse iuris divini, sed tantum humani" within the limitations placed by himself on the topic is recognized quite universally today. In fact, no vestige of that particular exemption now exists.

Navarrus (†1586) and Barbosa (†1649), among the canonists, really propsed an eclectic view. As has been seen, the former admitted that in spiritual matters and in criminal cases the clergy were exempt by divine law;[5] in regard to patrimonial goods, Navarrus drew a distinction between the goods of the Church and the private goods of the clergy—a distinction that was not made in the ecclesiastical legislation itself—and argued that the latter should not be placed on a par with the goods of

saecularium immunes esse."—*Practicarum quaestionum liber unus* ([ ] ed., Coloniae Allobrogum, 1679), cap. XXXI, nn. 2-4.

[4] *Ioannis Medinae de poenitentia, restitutione et contractibus praeclarum et absolutum opus in duos divisum tomos* (2 toms. in 1 vol., Ingolstadii, 1581), *Codex de rebus restituendis,* q. 15.

[5] *Supra,* p. 80.

the Church, and could in their immunity be subject to contrary legal prescription by immemorial custom whenever such custom had intervened, even though this was derogatory to ecclesiastical liberty.[6] Barbosa conceded that only in matters that are truly and properly spiritual could the exemption be considered as of divine law; the exemption in temporal matters, he agreed, was very much in accord with divine law, but not the object of a strict precept.[7]

Although the proponents of this view refused to admit a strict obligation in justice from the natural or divine law, nevertheless they agreed that there was every reason *in equity* for the exemption; they showed (with the exception of Joannes Medina) how apt was the expression of Bellarmine that "the canonists assert what the thoelogians do not deny." The single trend of Catholic thought, namely that immunities were not only of human right but of divine law as well, was exemplified in the writings of the latter both before and after the time of Bellarmine. Thus Dominicus Soto (†1560) observed that it is especially congruous according to divine law that there be *some exemption* accorded to the clergy, although it is *not fully conclusive* that there is a strict obligation in justice.[8] The very same conclusions were arrived at by Ludovicus Molina (†1600)[9] who quoted Cajetan (†1534) and Franciscus Victoria (†1546) in support of this view.

It was Leonardus Lessius (†1623), however, who first seems to have observed that this view, which he heartily endorsed, was reconcilable with those of the other school.[10] But just as the

[6] *Martini ab Azpilcueta doctoris navarri consiliorum sive responsorum libri V iuxta ordinem decretalium dispositi, comment.* in lib. III, tit. XLIX, *consilia* V, n. 3 & VI, n. 4.

[7] *Iuris ecclesiastici universi libri tres* ([ ] ed., Lugduni, 1659), lib. I, cap. XXXIX §§ 6-7.

[8] *Dominici Soto segobiensis in quartum (quem vocant) sententiarum tomus secundus* ([ ] ed., Ventiis, 1575), Comment. in quartam, dist. XXV, q. II, art. II, nn. 1-6.

[9] *Ludovici Moliane de iustitia et iure tomus primus de contractibus* ([ ] ed., Moguntiae, 1609), tract. II, disp. XXI, n.6

[10] As seen above; cf. *supra*, p. 81. It will be observed that Lessius' work

opposite school labored to show that the exemption in temporal matters was *in accordance with divine law,* so this group strove to prove to show that there was *no obligation in divine law.* Among the latter group the element of *justice* was emphasized; that of conformity with the divine law was secondary. Among the former the element of *conformity with the divine law* was primary; the element of strict justice was scarcely mentioned in this regard. Lessius, following Cajetan, Victoria, Medina, Molina, Soto and others, clearly held that there is no strict precept in justice in this matter, and adduced arguments that were quite as potent as those of his predecesor to prove that Scripture, tradition, natural reason and the testimony of the popes and councils could not be adduced to prove the existence of any such strict right.[11]

In company with his predecessors of the same school, Lessius placed the formal cause of clerical immunity in canon and civil law; nevertheless, he declared that, although the natural law does not effect the exemption, it *dictates* that it is to be made by princes by reason of the dignity of the clerical state, by virtue of the position of the clergy as fathers and judges of the laity

was already in its third edition in 1612. It may be that Lessius first pointed out the reconcilability of the two views and Bellarmine developed it. At all events, Lessius merely alluded to it; Belarmine made it the basis of his treatment. Yet they are sometimes placed at opposite poles. The difference between the treatment of the question by the theologians and by the canonists can be illustrated by the following quotation from Lessius: "Non sunt ita exempti iure divino, ut absque ulla alia exemptione nou sint subditi Prinicpibus saecularibus, sic ut Principes perccent contra iustitiam si de causis eorum temporalibus cognoscant, aut tributa ab ipsis exigant. Kecte tamen quadam ratione dici possunt Iure divino exempti, quodam lure Canonico et Civili . . . Principes lege religionis, observantiae et gratitudinis obligari, ut ecclesiasticos exemptos habeant seu eximant: non autem ipsam exemptionem immediate a Deo esse factam . . . Hoc modo videntur posse Canonistae cum Theologis reconciliari."—*De iustitia et iure caeterisque virtutibus cardinalibus,* lib. II, cap. XXXIII, dub. IV, nn. 28 & 36.

[11] "Talis exemptio probari potest neque ex sacris litteris, neque ex traditione, neque ex naturali ratione, neque Pontificum testimonio."—*loc. cit.,* n. 28.

and in view of the greater benefits that accrue to society by reason of the clerical offices.[12] Lessius' consistent use of the word ***dictates*** is an indication of how closely his view paralleled that of the canonists and exemplified the dictum of Bellarmine. What Bellarmine regarded as belonging to the third class of principles of the natural law (jus gentium), Lessius and the other theologians more correctly viewed as being *in accordance with the natural law,* without implying a strict obligation. The same word, *"dictates,"* was later employed by Felicianus de Oliva, a later canonist who shared this view and regarded it as (at least extrinsically) the more common and more probable opinion.[13] The position of Diana (†1663) who employed this same word, has been observed in the preceeding chapter as an illustration of the close proximity of the two views ***in fact***.[14]

Emmanuel Gonzalez-Tellez (†1649) seems to have geen more exact. He agreed with both sides that the exemption in spiritual matters is of divine law and observed that the power to exempt ecclesiastical persons and their cases from secular jurisdiction is of divine law; but held with the theologians that in criminal cases and clerical goods the exemption is of ***positive*** (sc. ecclesiastical) origin.[15]

[12] *Loc. cit.*, n. 30.

[13] "Secunda autem sententia est contraria asserens exemptionem quoad personas et res clericorum, non a iure Divino originem trahere immediatc, sed esse immediate a jure humano introducto . . . Licet contraria opinio [sc. de iure divino] sit valde probabilis et etiam satis communis inter jurisperitos, cum tamen talis non sit inter Theologos, haecque [sc. opinio de iure humano] sit tam Theologorum quam Jurisperitorum communis, magis recepta et communior redditur, et probabiliorem existimamus quia validioribus nititur fundamentis et fortioribus"—Feliciani de Oliva, *Tractatus de foro ecclesiae* (Coloniae Allobrogum, 1733), Pars I, q. X, n. 9.

[14] *Supra*, p. 82.

[15] This observation had been made by theologians; it does not seem to have been made by canonists. "In hoc interpretum dissidio placet sententia eorum, qui affirmant exemptionem ecclesiasticam quoad spiritualia negotia a jure divino positivo provenire; quoad causas vero criminales et bona clericorum a jure positivo originem trahere, licet potestas ipsa eximendi ecclesiasticas personas, eorumque causas a jurisdictione saeculari jure divino nitatur."—tom. II, *comment.* in c. 8, *de iudiciis,* I, II, n. 2.

It has been noted in the preceeding chapter that Ernricus Pirhing (†1679) observed that this view could be called *originaliter et initiative* of divine law, but rejected it on the grounds that the contrary opinion was "the more common view of canonists, more in conformity with canon law, more favorable to the clerical state, based upon better foundations and rightly to be preferred." [16] Nevertheless a later editor of Pirhing's work, without giving any hint as to what had been Pirhing's own view of the matter, employed these very words to indicate that this view, rejected by the author himself, had by 1849 so gained in popularity as to become by that time the more common opinion.[17]

The rôle which Franciscus Schmalzgrueber (†1735) seems to have played in building up its popularity will be discussed in the next chapter.

Article 2. The Arguments and Their Evaluation

The authors whose explanation has been presented in this chapter employed the very same arguments that have been already discussed in the preceeding chapter. The specific difference between the two schools, however, rests in their *mode of treatment.* The one stressed the conformity between clerical immunity and divine law, and with the exception of Suarez and a few others who insisted upon a strict right, did not go quite so far as to say explicitly that there is a strict right of clerical immunity in temporal matters in the natural or divine positive law itself;

[16] Pirhing, lib. II, tit. II, n. 112; cf. *supra,* pp. 83-84.

[17] "Qui clericos et alias personas ecclesiasticas iure divino, et naturali eximunt a laica potestate, et iurisdictione, multi sunt, et non levia fundamenta habent suae opinionis . . . His tamen nihil obstantibus, fatetur quidem communior sententia, originaliter iuris divini esse hanc clericorum exemptionem, eo quod scilicet Deus dederit summo pontifici hanc eximendi potestatem; et satis certum esse, quod si in rebus mere spiritualibus, et ecclesiasticis exemptio haec sit iuris divini formaliter, et immediate; clericorum tamen, et talium personarum exemptionem, formaliter, et immediate iuris esse positivi humani, tam canonici, quam civilis."—anonymous, *Synopsis pirhingiana seu ss. canonum doctrina ex fusioribus quinque libris Henrici* [sic] *Pirhing* (ed. novissima, Romae: 1849), lib. II, tit. II, § V.

the other group admitted that their arguments prove this, but stressed the fact that they are insufficient to demonstrate a strict right to clerical exemption by divine law. The difference between the two schools was in point of fact so slight that Bellarmine rightly observed that "the cannonists assert what the theologians do not deny." [18] Accordingly, the method of argumentation between the two schools was somewhat different. Those whose view is considered here employed both *negative arguments* to demonstrate the absence of any strict precept of divine law, as well as *positive proofs* to show the extreme suitability of clerical exemption in accordance with divine law. These positive proofs were in reality the same that had been employed by the other school, but with a more limited scope.

A. NEGATIVE ARGUMENTS

The primary concern of the canonists and theologians who employed these was to demonstrate that the immunity of the clergy in temporal matters could be demonstrated neither from Scripture, nor from the natural law, nor from the canonical texts themselves, regardless of how strongly in conformity with the natural law the exemption actually is.

§ 1. *The Argument from Scripture*

Regarding the precepts of the Old Testament [19] the writers mentioned in this group argued that these were ceremonial precepts and had been revoked by the law of the Gospel. The words of Christ in response to Peter's answer to His question on the occasion of the payment of the drachma to the temple, that the children of the kingdom are free from the payment of earthly tributes,[20] they pointed out, referred to natural sons and not to adopted sons; moreover, they agreed that this text proves the freedom of Christ Himself and perhaps of the apostles as well, but that it did not demonstrate the exemption of the clergy. For, if applied to them, it could be applied to the laity as well

[18] *De clericis,* lib. I, cap. XXVIII.

[19] Gen. XLVII, 22; Leviticus XL, 28; Numbers III, 10; I Esdras VII, 24.

[20] Matt. XVII, 23.

with equal justification.[21] On the other hand, these texts as well as others [22] were adduced to show that such examples and testimonies indicated the extreme suitability of clerical exemption in temporal matters, and that, although the Old Law is no longer in force, the exemption of which the Old Testament furnishes examples, is applied with greater reason to the clergy of the New Dispensation, whose dignity and sacred functions are incomparably greater and more sublime.[23]

§ 2. *The Argument from the Natural Law*

It must be remembered that as Bellarmine,[24] Suarez,[25] and several of the modern authors indicate,[26] many of the older Catholic writers did not clearly determine whether their arguments were intended to illustrate the natural law or the divine positive law. They seem to have employed them to illustrate the suitability of clerical exemption according to both sources. On the contrary the writers who developed this phase of immunity made use of the examples from Sacred Scripture in the Old Testament cumulatively with other arguments from the common practices of pre-Christian peoples to show the extreme conformity of clerical immunity with the natural law but the absence of a strict precept, on the one hand; and the revocation of the Old Testament, on the other, to indicate that whatever divine precept there may have been before the coming of Christ, was no longer in force after His advent. Medina contended that the testimonies of the Old Testament in this regard were not divine precepts at all, but were examples of human law and did not

[21] Covarruvias, *Practicarum quaestionum liber unus,* cap. XXXI, n. 5; de Oliva, *Tractatus de foro ecclesiastico,* q. 4, n. 15; Molina, *De iustitia et iure,* tom. I, tract. II, disp. XXXI, n. 6.

[22] E. g., Psalm CIV, 15.

[23] Covarruvias, de Oliva, Molina, *loc. citt.,* Soto, *Commentarium,* dist. XXV, q. II, art. II, n. 4; Lessius, *de iustitia et iure,* lib. II, cap. 33, dub. IV, n. 31.

[24] *De clericis,* lib. I, cap. XXX.

[25] *De immunitate ecclesiastica,* p. 389.

[26] E. g., Cappello, *Summa iuris publici ecclesiastici,* p. 457; Coronata, *Ius publicum ecclesiasticum,* p. 208.

entail the idea of complete exemption from the temporal jurisdiction of the civil authority.[27]

As expressed by Medina, this proposition would admit of a regalist interpretation. The other writers, however, admitted that there had been a precept in the Old Law, but contended that it was not one of the irrevocable moral precepts. Suarez, however, insisted that it belonged to the latter class and hence was still binding.[28]

All agreed, however, that the dignity of the clerical state, which is far superior to and infinitely more holy than either the priesthood of the Old Testament or that of the gentiles, at least urged that exemption from civil jurisdiction and from civil obligations be made by human law. The position of the clergy as fathers and judges of the faithful and the irreverence involved in the subjection of ecclesiastics to the laity, particularly in forensic matters, gave rise to a *strong* indication of the suitability of clerical exemption. Finally, the greater benefits which the clergy render to the State by reason of their divine offices, strongly suggested that their exemption from civil jurisdiction, if not strictly necessary, was at least very much in accord with the natural law. Other considerations were: that the clergy be more free to pursue the obligations attendant upon their sacred vocation, that it was desirable to avoid the incongruity and scandal that would arise from the indiscriminate subjection of the clergy to secular obligations and particularly to the jurisdiction of secular tribunals; and that the clerical state would be rendered contemptible in the eyes of men if its members who were especially dedicated to divine worship were subjected to duties which were not at all expedient to their salvation.[29]

The point which these writers commonly insisted upon, however, was that there exists no sufficient indication that clerical

[27] *Codex de restitutione*, q. XV.

[28] *De immunitate ecclesiastica*, pp. 400-401.

[29] Molina, *de iustitia et iure*, tom. I, tract. II, disp. XXXI, n. 7; de Oliva, *Tractatus de foro ecclesiae*, pars I, q. IX, nn. 15-16; Lessius, *de iustitia et iure*, lib. II, cap. 33, dub. IV, nn. 30-31; Soto, *Commentarium*, dist. XXV, q. II, art. II, n. 5.

exemption in temporal matters is of divine natural law any more than of divine positive law. They admitted, nevertheless, that there is abundant reason to believe that it is very much according to the spirit of the natural law, even though a precept from that precise title could not be urged. Thus Molina,[30] Felicianus de Oliva,[31] Leonardus Lessius,[32] Dominicus Soto,[33] as well as the other writers cited by them, concur that, despite the extreme suitability of clerical exemption according to divine law, both natural and positive, nevertheless there exists no strict precept in either of these fonts which would postulate such immunity.

§ 3. *The Conclusions of This School in Regard to Canonical Texts*

As has been observed in the preceding chapter, the expressions contained in the decretals and reiterated in the general councils after the promulgation of the same stated that clerical immunity is not only of human law, but of divine law as well.[34] The group of writers mentioned in this chapter realized that it was not necessary to conclude that these texts implied that all clerical exemption from the civil power is formally and immediately of divine law. This school referred the expression *divine law* to immunity in spiritual matters only; and, with regard to temporal matters, agreed to the extreme suitability of their immunity *in accordance with the natural or divine positive law,* but pointed out that no strict precept could be proved in the case of these. Thus de Oliva,[35] Molina and Soto,[36] together with Lessius,[37]

[30] *De iustitia et iure,* tom. I, tract. II, disp. XXXI, n. 6.

[31] *Tractatus de foro ecclesiae,* pars I, q. IX, n. 14.

[32] *De iustitia et iure,* lib. II, cap. 33, dib. IV, n. 28.

[33] *Commentarium,* dist. XXV, q. II, art. II, nn. 3-5.

[34] Cf. *supra,* p. 91.

[35] "Respondetur quod textus non magis hanc exemptionem tribuant juri divino quam humano, imo contra praedictam opinionem retorqueri possunt, cum docent etiam iure humano Clericos et eorum res exemptas esse, respondetur etiam et clarius, haec jura nihil concludere adversus hanc opinionem. Exemptio quoad spiritualia procedat de jure Divino, in quo omnes consentiunt: quoad temporalia vero quod ibi verba referenda sunt ad jus Divinum, secundum quod data est potestas Ecclesiae ad hanc exemptionem introducendam."—*Tractatus de foro ecclesiae,* pars I, q. X, n. 17.

agreed that this is the best explanation of the statements of the canonical texts; and it was Lessius who observed that the diversity between the two schools was the result of two different views of the same subject—a discrepancy that was more apparent than real.

B. POSITIVE ARGUMENTS

The explanation that clerical immunity from civil jurisdiction is not formally of divine law was supported by positive arguments in addition to the negative proofs that have just been examined. In general, Molina, Lessius, Gonzalez-Tellez, de Oliva, Covarruvias and the other writers already cited argued in this manner: the natural law, Scripture and the history of clerical exemption prove that immunity in temporal matters arose from human law alone. This argument refers to the natural law in the strict sense; it observes that what is contrary to divine law is never lawful. It then shows that, in fact, the subjection of the clergy to secular authority in temporal matters is proved by Scripture, tradition and reason. Accordingly, this subjection cannot be contrary to divine law; and hence immunity in temporal affairs cannot be contrary to divine law, but must be ascribed formally to human law.

§ 1. *The Argument from Scripture.*

From the New Testament were adduced the testimonies of St. Peter [38] and St. Paul,[39] as well as the example of St. Paul's own appeal to Caesar against his accusation by the Jews,[40] in support of the contention that the immunity of the clergy cannot be considered to be formally of divine law in view of the testimonies and examples of these texts. As treated by the writers mentioned in this chapter, these arguments were hardly more than mentioned as parts of a cumulative chain. Their treatment by these writers must be sharply differentiated from that adopted by

[36] Molina, *De iustitia et iure,* tom. I, tract. II, disp. XXXI, n. 14.

[37] *De iustitia et iure,* lib. II, cap. 33, dub. IV, n. 32.

[38] I Peter II, 13-14.

[39] Rom. XIII, 1-2.

[40] Acts XXV, 10.

the regalists who sought by the use of these texts to prove the subjection of the Church to the State. Any such interpretation has always been far from the minds of Catholics whose orthodoxy is to remain unquestioned. St. Peter's words: "Be ye subject therefore to every human creature for God's sake: whether it be to the king as excelling; or to governors as sent by him for the punishment of evildoers, and for the praise of the good;"[41] together with St. Paul's admonition: "Let every soul be subject to the higher powers: for there is no power but from God. Therefore he that resisteth the power resisteth the ordinance of God;" and the latter's appeal to the king: "I stand at Caesar's judgment seat where I ought to be judged;" [42] were presented as corroborative proof rather than as distinct arguments in support of the teaching that clerical immunity in temporal affairs is simply not of divine law.[43]

Against the introduction of these texts, however, Bellarmine, Suarez and others replied that the testimony proves nothing more than that all men are subject to their legitimate superiors; but submitted the objection that the subjection of the clergy to civil authorities as their lawful superiors remains to be proved. Against it they raised the objection that Scripture also proves that no man can serve two masters.[44] This text, they averred, proved that the only legitimate superior for a cleric was his ecclesiastical superior, inasmuch as clerics were released from subjection to all temporal jurisdiction.[45] The appeal of St. Paul to Caesar was alleged to indicate that clerical exemption is not simply of divine law, since St. Paul would not have made the appeal if he were convinced that the secular courts had no jurisdiction over him. To this argument Suarez and Bellarmine

[41] I Peter II, 13-14.

[42] Rom. XIII, 1-2; Acts XXV, 10.

[43] Dominicus Soto, Ludovicus Molina, Leonardus Lessius, Felicianus de Oliva, Didacus Covarruvias, *locc. citt.*, who offered no further comment regarding these texts.

[44] Matt. VI, 24.

[45] Bellarmine, *De clericis*, lib. I, cap. 30; Suarez, *De immunitate ecclesiastica*, p. 397.

replied that Paul's appeal was *de facto* not *de iure;* that St. Paul had appealed to the imperial throne only because he was constrained to do so by the calumnies of the Jews and the injustice of the Roman governor, who recognized no king but Caesar.[46] It must be recalled, however, that Bellarmine admitted that no strict obligation of clerical immunity in temporal affairs could be proved from the pages of Holy Writ; he pointed out, however, that their exemption could be deduced by a probable consequence from Scripture,[47] despite the objections to this view that had been raised from the pages of Scripture.

§ 2. *The Argument from the Natural Law.*

This argument, as it was presented by the theologians and those canonists who emphasised the absence of any divine precept for the exemption of the clergy from secular jurisdiction in temporal affairs, admitted that the honor and dignity of the clerical state, and the infinitely greater service which the clergy render to the State make it eminently fitting that their immunity be observed. It pointed out, nevertheless, that the clerical state in itself is insufficient to exempt a person from civil jurisdiction on that score alone. In other words, it submitted that there is no repugnance in the concept that one can be especially dedicated to divine cult and at the same time subject to a temporal prince in temporal matters. De Oliva pointed out that, despite their special consecration to God, the clergy are none the less capable of performing merely temporal actions, and that therefore the clerical state by itself, apart from any other consideration, is insufficient to postulate complete clerical immunity.[48] Bartholomeus Medina observed that Franciscus Victoria and Dominicus Soto

[46] Bellarmine and Suarez, *locc. citt.*

[47] "Nos per jus divinum non intelligimus praeceptum Dei proprie dictum, quod extet expresse in Sacris Scripturis, sed quod ab exemplis vel testimoniis testamenti veteris et novi per quamdam similitudinem deduci possit. Atque hisce fortasse conciliari poterunt Theologorum et juris peritorum sententiae. Illi enim cum negant, exemptionem Clericorum esse juris divini, praeceptum divinum proprie dictum expresse in Scripturis extare negant."—*De clericis,* lib. I, cap. XXVIII; cf. capp. XXIX-XXX.

[48] *Tractatus de foro ecclesiae,* pars I, q. X, n. 20.

had explained this matter so clearly that further comment from himself was unnecessary, and referred his readers to these authors.[49] Dominicus Soto argued that, notwithstanding their clerical character, the clergy remain citizens and members of the republic, although they are not bound by its coercive power.[50] Covarruvias alleged in support of this argument what had been admitted by Suarez and Bellarmine, namely that divine law alone aside from its human constitution would be insufficient to prove clerical exemption.[51]

Lessius, on the other hand, seems to have regarded civil and canon law as already bound by natural law to decree the exemption of the clergy. At the beginning of his treatise he agreed that clerical exemption in temporal affairs cannot be proved from natural reason.[52] Nevertheless his consistent use of the word *dictat* throughout his treatise carries a stronger connotation than the expressions employed by other authors of this school.[53] He concluded his argument against the immediate exemption of the clergy as a matter of justice according to the natural law, by observing that, nevertheless, princes are *bound* by the law of religion, respect and gratitude to exempt the clergy, but that this exemption is *not immediately* of divine right.[54] The position of Lessius illustrates *only a verbal distinction* from the view of even the most rigorous proponents of the contrary view.[55]

[49] Bartholomeus à Medina, *Expositio in primam secundae Angelici doctoris D. Thomae Aquinatis* (3. ed., Venetiis, 1590), ad art. VI, 517.

[50] *Commentarium,* dist. XXV, q. II, art. II, n. 5.

[51] "Atque ideo, si iure divino absque humanis constitutionibus res esset examinanda, respondendum foret, in hisce temporalibus, nec clericos, nec eorum res a iurisdictione saeculari immunes esse."—*Practicarum quaestionum liber unus,* cap. XXXI, n. 2.

[52] *De iustitia et iure,* lib. II, cap. 33, dub. IV, n. 28.

[53] This has been observed above; cf. *supra,* pp. 100-101.

[54] "Ex his patet, Principes lege religionis, observantiae et gratitudinis obligari, ut ecclesiasticos habeant exemptos seu eximant: non autem ipsam exemptionem immediate a Deo factam."—*loc. cit.,* n. 30.

[55] "Quod iure Canonico et Civili exempti sint reipsa, probatur, quia quod ius Divinum naturale dictabat esse faciendum, id Iure Canonico et Civili praestitum est."—*loc. cit.,* n. 33; "Iure divino naturali Principes tenentur eam facere, et factam ratam habere."—*loc. cit.,* n. 35.

§ 3. *The Argument from the History of Clerical Immunity*

The best proof that clerical exemption does not formally exist by virtue of divine law but is to be ascribed to human law has been the argument from the history of clerical immunity itself. If it can be demonstrated that the clergy were subject to civil jurisdiction at any time in the history of the Church, their exemption cannot be ascribed formally to divine law. Covarruvias, Lessius, Molina, de Oliva and others of this school[56] adduced many instances designed to show that the immunity of the clergy could not be ascribed to divine law on the ground that, during the first three centuries of the Christian era there could be no question of immunity, due to the fact that the Church itself was a proscribed society; that clerical exemption came about gradually; and that any change in ecclesiastical discipline would militate against the consideration that clerical immunity in temporal affairs could be formally of divine law. These objections were answered by those who held the contrary opinion, who pointed out that the denial of clerical immunity during the era of the pagan emperors was *de facto* and not *de iure;* that although circumstances made it impossible for the Church to exercise her right in this regard, her right existed none the less; that the gradual recognition of clerical immunity by Christian emperors simply proved that not every species of immunity is formally of divine law; and that changes in discipline in the legislation of the canons did not militate against the divine right of the Church to make changes in the establishment, protection and derogation of clerical immunity—either directly or indirectly —by the law of the Church.

Article 3. Conclusion

The assertions and contradictions made by the two schools of Catholic writers, as outlined above, indicate not that there was an impassé on any essential point in the matter of the juridical origin of clerical immunity, but that both groups considered two distinct phases of the same question. Neither Bellarmine, Suarez,

[56] *Locc. citt.*

Joannes Dreido, Hostiensis or anyone else pretended that clerical immunity in temporal matters had not been introduced by civil and ecclesiastical constitutions; they did aver, however, that it was not lacking some element of divine law as well. On the other hand, Covarruvias, Dominicus Soto, Medina, de Oliva and the others who belonged to their school, agreed in granting the extreme suitability and conformity of clerical immunity with the natural law, the testimony of gentile customs and the pages of Holy Writ. Lessius went so far as to indicate that civil and ecclesiastical law may have been already bound by natural law in this matter. Their point was that *formally and immediately* immunity in secular affairs could not be directly ascribed to divine law, regardless of how suitable the exemption may be. That both sides admitted the concordance as well as the probability of the contrary view in this sense, is evidence that they were considering the same question from two different viewpoints.

Thus Joannes Dreido, who, with Bellarmine, ascribed the exemption of ecclesiastics from tributes imposed by the secular authority not only to human law, but to divine law as well by reason of the fact that even kings are obliged to submit to ecclesiastical jurisdiction, refused to admit that this particular immunity arose merely from mere royal concessions.[57] This did not substantially contradict Lessius, who interpreted St. Thomas' employment of the term *natural equity* as an indication that this exemption was *not in itself necessary* according to strict natural law.[58] Dominicus Soto[59] and Covarruvias[60] supported the conclusion of Lessius, as did de Oliva, who observed that regardless of the pope's power to exempt the clergy from civil jurisdiction, if clerical immunity were formally of divine law, it could not be changed by canon law, and concluded that in view of the considerations from the nature and history of clerical immunity as

[57] *De libertate christiana liber,* p. 110.

[58] "D. Thomas dicit exemptionem ecclesiasticorum a tributis habere naturalem aequitatem, non tamen ex necessitate, quasi sit de iure divino." —*De iustitia et iure,* lib. II, cap. 33, disp. IV, n. 28.

[59] *Comment.,* dist. XXV, q. II, art. II, n. 3.

[60] *Practicarum quaestionum liber unus,* cap. XXXI, n. 7.

well as from an examination of the texts from Sacred Scripture, the privilege of clerical exemption is not formally and immediately of divine, but of human law.[61]

Modern authors are inclined to present their evaluation of this view not according to the manner in which the older authors themselves presented it, but as a criticism of the statement that clerical immunity is simply not of divine but is only of human law. They distinguish this opinion from that of regalists; they are not inclined to say just who proposed it in its absolute form, i.e., without indicating that there is at least some suitability according to the divine law. Perhaps Covarruvias, Joannes Medina or Felicianus de Oliva would be subject to this criticism if their conclusion alone are examined; even these authors, however escape it when their explanation of the entire question is observed. Thus de Angelis rightly interpreted the view as expressed by Lessius, when he pointed out that this opinion established the *suitability* of clerical immunity from the natural law.[62] Cappello, on the contrary, rejected it on the ground that it leaves no room for the suitability and natural equity upon which clerical immunity is based.[63] It is true that Joannes Medina accorded scant attention to the suitability of clerical immunity in his treatise on the question; nevertheless, in company with all the other writers who have been consulted, he did mention it. In actual fact, only one writer could be found who expressed himself in the manner censured by Cappello. This was Petrus Leurenius (†1723), who, however, seems to have indicated that he rejected the view that the natural law in the strict sense which would obtain the implication of an obligation could be considered as basic element of clerical immunity.[64]

[61] "Ergo privilegium non est de jure divino, sed humano."—De Oliva, *Tractatus de foro ecclesiae,* pars I, q. X, nn. 11-13.

[62] De Angelis, lib. III, tit. XLIX, n. 2.

[63] "Alii tenent esse iuris *ecclesiastici* tantum, quia non constat de iure divino sive naturali sive positivo, eoque admisso explicari non possent plures variationes . . . Quare ex facto *convenientiae* sive aequitatis naturalis refellitur tertia opinio."—*Summa iuris publici ecclesiastici,* pp. 457-458.

[64] "Non de iure naturali, attendenda sunt tamen privilegia et legitimae

More correctly in accord with the actual expression of the older writers themselves, Cavagnis declined to consider this view as substantially different from the common opinion. Ottaviani is content to reprove only those who, without reserve (*modo absoluto*) would proclaim that clerical immunity is *only* of ecclesiastical or of civil law; he points out that such a stand would not provide a sufficient explanation of the ecclesiastical documents regarding the juridical nature of clerical immunity.[65] Coronata seems to come closer than the others to an appreciation of just what the older proponents of this view actually did teach regarding the place that divine law holds as a basis of clerical immunity. He observes that the arguments in favor of this opinion are not to be disregarded, and recognizes the fact that although this view rightly declines to accept a divine precept of clerical immunity, nevertheless it does not exclude in its general assertion what the common opinion holds regarding the foundation of clerical immunity in divine law.[66]

It is of the utmost importance to differentiate the view of the

consuetudines Principum . . . et idem dicendum [est] in tota materia de Immunitate Ecclesiastica."—*Forum ecclesiasticum in quo ius canonicum universum librorum ac titulorum ordine explanatur* (5 vols., Moguntiae, 1717-1735), lib. III, tit. XLIX, cap. 4, q. MLI.

65 "Sunt igitur, tertium, nonnulli qui considerantes non posse admitti, modo absoluto, tamquam titulum et causam immunitatum sive ius divinum sive ex adverso ius civile, concludunt immunitates *e iure ecclesiastico* esse repetendas; quod sane confirmant ex variis mutationibus quas, temporum decursu, unice ex tolerantia vel positiva approbatione Ecclesiae, immunitates passae sunt. *Sed* haec opinio, si modo absoluto proferatur, non potest certe se expedire ab efficacia difficultatum quae in contrarium opponuntur, ex documentis auctoritatis ecclesiasticae."—*Institutiones iuris publici ecclesiastici*, I, 404.

66 "Tertia opinio docet omnes immunitates esse *formaliter ex iure canonico*. Hanc theoriam . . . probant ex eo quod praeceptum divinum quo immunitates statuuntur et determinantur probari non possit . . . Argumenta, quibus haec opinio innuitur, non sunt certe spernenda, nec ipsa excludit in sua generali assertione id quod affirmat quarta opinio de fundamento immunitatum in iure divino."—*Ius publicum ecclesiasticum*, pp. 208-209. Even this statement, however, in the light of the quotations submitted in this chapter, tends to undevaluate the presentation of the case by the older authors.

writers mentioned in this chapter from that of the regalists, both Protestant and Catholic, who assigned all clerical immunity in its origin, constitution and abrogation to the mere good-will of the civil authority.[67] The view was reprobated just as strongly by Catholic writers of the school that saw no strict precept of clerical immunity in divine law as it was by those who disagreed with this particular presentation of the question. The purpose of this and the preceeding chapter has been to show that the contrariety between the two orthodox schools is more apparent than real. In addition to the employment of a diverse terminology, each group was concerned with a different view of the question. In great measure the disagreement between the writers discussed in these two chapters is paradoxical: a contradiction appears when the statement of the question by both schools is contrasted; the contradiction disappears when the question and the arguments of both schools are examined. They represent two different views of the same subject. Each had its own case to prove; and each actually accepted the conclusions of the other in the sense intended. What both resented was the exaggeration of one or the other view. Bellarmine's dictum that *the canonists assert what the theologians do not deny,* together with his explanation of just what he understood by *divine law* in this matter is the key which unlocks the paradox regarding the judicial origin of clerical immunity.[68]

It must be remembered that Suarez and Bellarmine were primarially controversialists; their arguments were written in answer to the Protestants and schismatics who, following the doctrines of Marsilius of Padua and John of Jandun, of Wycliffe and Hus, denied that clerical exemption in any sense could be ascribed to divine law. Suarez, it must be admitted, actually did hold that immunity in temporal matters proceeded formally and immediately in all rigor from divine law; however, he conceded the probability of the opposite opinion. No Catholic theologian or canonist worthy of the name can be found who would ascribe immunity without restriction to the mere good pleasure of the civil power;

[67] The view of the regalists has been discussed in chap. VI.
[68] *De clericis,* lib. I, cap. XXVIII.

such an opinion is contrary to divine law inasmuch as it would limit the power of the Church over the clergy; it is contrary to the obvious words of the canons, and is now formally condemned in propositions 30, 31 and 32 of the *Syllabus errorum* of Pope Pius IX.

In conclusion, the paradox can be explained by observing that Bellarmine, Suarez and others of their school were speaking of immunity in general; their points of departure were that exemption in spiritual matters is of divine law; the power of the Church to decree clerical exemption extends even to secular affairs; the reasons why the Church has established the immunity of the clergy are founded in the natural law and follow the precedent of the examples and testimonies of the Old Testament. Navarrus, Barbosa, Covarruvias, Gonzalez-Tellez, Altessera, de Oliva and the theologians whose view has been scrutinized in the first part of this chapter, on the other hand, were concerned primarily with pointing out that, regardless of the basis of the reasons persuasive of clerical immunity or its extreme suitability according to divine law, clerical exemption from civil jurisdiction in temporal matters is *formally, immediately* and *specifically* of human law, civil and ecclesiastical.

Chapter VIII.

THE RISE AND GROWTH OF THE *OPINIO MEDIA*

The differences of opinion that have been discussed in the two preceding chapters represented a sincere attempt on the part of theologians and canonists to establish the juridical basis of clerical immunity in temporal matters according to the language and spirit of Christian tradition as exemplified in the decrees of the popes and councils. These differences were in fact not as radical as they appear at first sight. They might be called trends toward one direction or the other, rather than sharply defined categories. An interesting parallel can be observed between the presentation of the case by Bellarmine (†1621) and Lessius (†1623) in the seventeenth century on the one hand, and by Vitus Pichler (†1736) and Franciscus Schmalzgrueber (†1735) in the eighteenth century on the other. Bellarmine and Pichler represent what would correspond to the approach from the viewpoint of divine law; Lessius and Schmalzgrueber represent the approach from the viewpoint of human law. But where both Bellarmine and Lessius observed that the "canonists assert what the theologians do not deny," the writers of the following century, although they were in substantial agreement, can be observed to have been working towards a clearer expression of the juridical origin of clerical immunity.

Article 1. Presentation of the Question

Vitus Pichler observed that no Catholic could deny that *in some way* the immunity of ecclesiastical persons was derived from divine law, and observed that those Catholic authors who denied this proposition as stated, are to be understood as denying only that immunities proceed *immediately* from divine law, for all admitted that *mediately* and *basically* they were of divine law inasmuch as Christ gave His Church the power to exempt the clergy from the secular forum and constituted them fathers and teachers of the faithful.[1] His own opinion of the state of the

[1] "Ergo nullus inficias Catholicorum ivêrit, saltem *aliquo modo* Juris

question, however, was more in accord with the explanation that had been given by Pirhing and Reiffenstuel. In order further to clarify his position, Pichler introduced the expression *jure divino in thesi, jure humano in hypothesi,* which he explained as indicating that prescinding from particular cases and circumstances, clerical immunity can be considered of divine law, the application and specification of which is the peculiar function of ecclesiastical law.[3] This expression was employed by many other writers, among whom can be noted Maschat a S. Erasmo (†1747)[4] and Placidus Böchn (†1752),[5] who, nevertheless, admitted that this cannot be proved by Holy Writ and that the usual objections could be urged against it. His conclusion was that this is the best explanation of the canonical declarations concerning clerical immunity.[6]

Divini esse immunitatem personarum Ecclesiasticarum. Unde, quando Catholici DD. plurimi eam Juris Divini esse negant cum Covarruv., Molina, Farinacia, Oliva, intelligendi veniunt in eo sensu, quod dicta immunitas non *immediate* descendat a Jure Divino, sed solum mediate, originaliter et initiative, quatenus nempe Christus dedit Ecclesiae mandatum eximendi Clericos et Religiosos a foro saeculari, vel quatenus Clericos constituit velut Patres et Magistros reliquorum fidelium."—Pichler, lib. II, tit. II, n. 8.

[3] "Addidi tamen, *in thesi,* h. e. in genere, seu secundum rationem genericam, et abstrahendo a casibus et circumstantiis particularibus, vel ab hypothesi particulari, et applicatione ad materias, causas, circumstantias specificas aut individuales, adeoque *in hypothesi,* declarare ad Ecclesiam pertinet, an hic et nunc, atque in particularibus casibus illud generale privilegium, a Deo et Christo immediate concessam, habeat locum, nec ne." —Pichler, lib. II, tit. II, n. 8.

[4] "Formaliter iuris divini saltem in thesi, seu genere, licet determinatio illius quod particulares circumstantias et personas dependat a vicario Christi."—Remigius Maschat a S. Erasmo, *Institutiones canonicae* (2 toms., Romae, 1757), lib. II, tit. II, n. 23.

[5] "Censemus autem probabilius, Clericos Jure Divino, immo et naturali *in thesi loquendo,* a jurisdictione et foro laico liberos esse."—*Commentarius in jus canonicum universum sive in quinque libros decretalium Gregorii IX pont. max* (3 toms., Salisburgi, 1776), lib. II, tit. II, n. 64.

[6] "Quidquid sacrum est, Juri divino subjacet jurisdictioni et potestati Pontificiae non Regiae. Atqui personae Clericorum non minus, sed magis sunt sacrae, quam aliae Deo dicatae res. Ergo et personae Clericorum

The expression that clerical immunity is ***immediate juris humani, originaliter tamen et initiative juris divine*** had been rejected by Pirhing, Reiffenstuel, Pichler and the other authors mentioned. Schmalzgrueber observed that this was really the teaching of Lessius, Gonzalez-Tellez and others, although he stated that the expression iself had not been employed by them. Schmalzgrueber, however, assigned Molina to the opposite view, although there is hardly any diversity between the teaching of Molina and that of Lessius and the other theologians. At all events, Schmalzgrueber presented this more precise expression of the juridical origin of clerical immunity as a third opinion—a *via media.* He pointed out that clerical exemption is immediately of human law, but that its basis in divine law according to the statement of the Council of Trent rests in the fact that it was introduced in imitation of the Old Law; that it is derived from a special instinct and to some extent a divine precept; and that although the law of nature does not necessarially demand that clerical exemption in temporal matters be observed, it is however very much in conformity with the law of nature that the clergy, who are dedicated to God, be not treated in the same manner as the laity. Moreover the Holy Father, who has power to govern the Church by divine law, can do what is especially in conformity with the divine and natural law.[7] With Schmalzgrueber, then, the statement of the question received a clearer formulation, even though the expression itself was not accepted by several of his contemporaries. This formulation, namely that the clergy in

Jure Divino sunt immunes a Principibus vel Judicibus saecularibus."—Böeckn, lib. II, tit. II, nn. 64 & 68.

[7] "Tenenda videtur sententia inter utramque priorem media . . . 1. Quia facta est [exemptio in temporalibus] ad imitationem legis antiquae. 2. Quia ex speciali quoddam instinctu et quodammodo praecepto Dei profecta est. 3. Quia etsi jure naturae non necessario competat clericis, tamen eidem maxime consentaneum est clericos, tamquam res Deo dicatas, non eodem modo tractari, sicut tractantur laici. Habet autem pontifex ex jure divino potestatem, gubernandi ecclesiam, et faciendi in illa, quod maxime consentaneum est juri divino et naturali: ergo etc. neque plus probant argumenta utriusque sententiae."—Schmalzgrueber, lib. II, tit. II, n. 98; cf. lib. III, tit. XLIX, n. 58.

temporal matters are not formally and immediately exempt from civil jurisdiction and from civil obligations by divine law, but formally and immediately by ecclesiastical and civil law, with a basis, however, (*originaliter, remote et mediate*) in divine law, has become the common opinion. It is a true *via media* between the extreme view of the regalists and the opinion of Suarez; with regard to other Catholic doctors, however, it seems to be little more than a clearer mode of expression, and once again illustrates Bellarmine's observation that one school asserts what the other does not deny.

Jacobus Zallinger (†1813) pointed out that the expression *in genere seu in thesi iuris divini* involved a certain inconsistency and was open to misinterpretation, inasmuch as each individual form or species of immunity is not formally of divine law, yet that which is predicted of the genus should also be predicable of each species within the genus,[8] and observed that the divisions or points which comprise immunity are distinct—some are formally of divine law, others are of human law—and that no conclusion can be drawn from one to the other, inasmuch as one or another can be abolished without violence being done to all immunity. The *articles* or points of clerical immunity which are immediately of divine law he rightly limited to those which concern the liberty and independence of the Church with regard to spiritual and sacred causes and to the power of the Church to regulate the life of her ministers; immunity in temporal affairs, he admitted, was immediately established by the canons and laws of Christian princes, although he observed that canon law was in no way dependent upon civil law in this matter.[9] Thus, in his understanding of the concept, Zallinger used the term immunity in the broad sense, and included native rights which are essential for the liberty of the Church as well as immunities in the strict sense of exemptions from civil obligations in temporal matters.

It has been observed that the apparent dissension among

[8] *Institutiones juris ecclesiastici maxime privati ordine decretalium* (5 vols., Romae, 1823), lib. II, tit. II, n. 70, note *q*.

[9] Zallinger, lib. II, tit. II, nn. 70-71.

Catholic authors regarding the precise statement of the juridical origin of clerical immunity has been hampered by the lack of a univocal terminology. Some employed the term *immunity* in the strict sense of exemptions from civil law in temporal matters; others employed it in the wider sense of all exemption from secular jurisdiction whether it be in strictly spiritual matters or in temporal affairs as well. The question is of value only in the field of public law, inasmuch as those authors whose primary concern is to present the private law assume that the right of the Church to establish immunity is of divine law. From the viewpoint of private law, it is sufficient to say that clerical immunity in matters temporal is of human ecclesiastical law; but the basis of this, namely the power of the Church to effect this exemption, as well as the reasons for it, are necessary in order to have a precise statement in public law of the juridical origin of clerical immunity.

Cappello rightly observes that the disagreement among Catholic authors on this point is verbal rather than real, and pleads for a more uniform expression among authors.[10] Coronata echoes this *desideratum*[11] and observes that although the terminology is still somewhat fluctuating, it seems to be tending towards a clear separation between the idea of immunity in the strict sense and that of native right.[12]

Article 2. The Common Opinion Today

Recent authors are in substantial agreement regarding the

10 "Itaque, mature omnibus consideratis, dicendum est dissensum inter catholicos potius in verbis et nominibus, quam in re reperiri.

"Valde optandum est, ut DD. catholici, accurate ac dilucide exposita doctrina, omnes eadem *terminologia* utantur, sicque cesset apparens dissensus."—*Summa iuris publici ecclesiastici,* p. 459.

11 Quaestio de natura iuridica immunitatum ecclesiasticarum non recte, ut videtur, posita est ab auctoribus, ex eo praecipue, quia notio univoca immunitatis ecclesiasticae, apud omnes auctores, desideratur, quo fit, ut catholici doctores re quidem plerumque conveniant, dissentiant autem terminis."—*Ius publicum ecclesiasticum,* pp. 210-211.

12 "Immo et terminologia licet aliquatenus fluctuans adhuc sit, tamen huc tendere iam videtur ut clare secernantur immunitates ecclesiasticae a iuribus nativis Ecclesiae."—*Ius publicum ecclesiasticum,* p. 215.

juridical origin of clerical immunity. Differences can be noted, however, in the expression of the common and true doctrine by the various writers. A bird's-eye view of the statements of canonists both prior and subsequent to the promulgation of the Code reveals that the conflict is more apparent than real.

Cardinal Soglia (†1855) presented both opinions, but inclined towards what had been the old "view of the canonists" that clerical immunity in civil affairs and criminal matters is of divine law.[13] Franciscus Santi (†1885) inclined to the opposite view.[14] This expression of the *opinio media,* which Santi recognized that it was, found expression in the works of Vecchiotti (c.1867),[15] Makeé (after 1897),[16] and De Angelis (†1881), who observed with Schmalzgrueber that this was the view of Lessius.[17] Ojetti (†1932), however, showed a tendency to revert to the expression *in genere sive in confuso iuris divini,* (but formally) *de iure ecclesiastico applicante et determinante ius divinum.*[18] E. Grandclaude (†1900), employed the terminology of Schmalzgrueber,[19] which differed only slightly from that expressed by

[13] "At vero qui contra sentiunt, asseruntque exemptionem Clericorum etiam in civilibus negotiis et criminalibus ad jus divinum referendum esse, ii quidem validioribus armis pugnare videntur."—*Institutiones iuris publici ecclesiastici libri III* (5. ed., Parisiis, 1853), lib. III, § 58.

[14] "Privilegium huiusmodi institutum fuisse et determinatum a lege positiva Ecclesiae, quae tamen fundatur in intentione juris divini et naturalis."—*Praelectiones juris canonici* (2. ed., 5 vols., in 3, Ratisbonnae, Neo-Eboracensis et Cincinatii, 1892), lib. II, tit. II, n. 27; lib. III, tit. XLIX, n. 16.

[15] *Institutiones canonicae* (19. ed., 3 vols., Augustae Taurinorum, 1886), I, 408.

[16] *Institutiones juris ecclesiastici tum publici tum privati* (2 toms., Parisiis, 1897), I, 94.

[17] De Angelis, lib. III, tit. XLIX, n. 2.

[18] *Synopsis rerum moralium et iuris pontificii* (Romae, 1899), v. *Immunitas personalis.*

[19] "Fundamentaliter, seu initiative seu originaliter juris divini et naturalis, dum formaliter esset juris humani. Haec sententia, quae sic explicata vix differt a secunda, videtur conformis traditioni et praxi Ecclesiae."—*Jus canonicum juxta ordinem decretalium* (4 toms., Parisiis, 1882), lib. II, tit. I, sect. III, n. II.

J. Gignac, whose words were similar to those used by Santi.[20] Cardinal Cavagnis (†1906) gave perhaps the most concise formulation to the question.[21] Liberatore (†1907), was in substantial agreement with this expression.[22]

Among the authors who wrote after the Code the same unity of doctrine and variety of expression can be observed. There seems to be no real problem today regarding the juridical origin of clerical immunity, apart from the diversity of terminology. Thus Ferreres,[23] Badii,[24] Maroto (†1937),[25] De Meester,[26] and Toso[27] correctly align the relative rôles of divine and ecclesiastical

[20] "Immunitates proveniunt a lege positiva Ecclesiae, quae tamen fundatur in intentione juris divini et naturalis."—*Compendium juris canonici de personis* (Quebec, 1901), p. 133; cf. p. 123.

[21] "Origo iuridica harum immunitatum est remote a iure divino, proxime a iure ecclesiastico."—*Institutiones iuris publici ecclesiastici,* II, 184.

[22] *Droit public de l'eglise* (ed. A. Onclàir, Paris, 1888), p. 332.

[23] "Immunitas haec [fori] sicut et ceterae tamquam ultimo fundamento innititur iuri divino, quo Pontificis necessaria potestas ad aptum regnum et gubernationem Ecclesiae data est et consequenter ad ea decernenda, quae opus erat, ut clerici reverentia statui eorum debita exciperentur. Immediate innuitur iuri canonico."—*Institutiones canonicae iuxtra novissimum codicem Pii X* (2. ed., 2 vols., Romae, 1920), I, 101-102.

[24] Attamen est doctrina catholica *immunitates ecclesiasticas non esse solum ex iure civili aut politica quadam conditione repetendas sed generatim spectatas ex ipso iure divino derivari."—Institutiones iuris canonici* (3. ed., Florentiae: Libreria Editrice Fiorentina, 1921), p. 97.

[25] "Immunitates generice sumptas fundamentum habere in iure divino, formaliter tamen ab Ecclesia procedere, ut Conc. Lat. V, sess. IX, et Conc. Trid., sess. XXV, c. 20 de ref., aperte affimare videntur."—*Institutiones iuris canonici ad normam novi codicis* (3. ed., 2 vols., Romae: apud Commentarium pro Religiosis, 1921), I, 559.

[26] "In hac igitur sententia immunitas clericorum profecta est a jure naturali et divino suadente et inducente, a jure ecclesiastico determinante, et a jure civili et gentium obsequente."—*Juris canonici et juris canonico-civilis compendium* (3 toms. in 4, Brugis, 1921-1928), I, 244.

[27] "Est igitur immunitas ecclesiastica Dei ordinatione et canonicis sanctionibus constituta. *Dei ordinatione* nempe quoad fundamentum, quod in natura positum est . . . Sed et *canonicis sanctionibus*: nam id quod in divino quidem iure fundatum, sed ab eodem iure expresse et plene non definitur, Ecclesiae est constituere pro temporum ac circumstantiarum varietate. Ideoque singulae leges quae de clericorum immunitatibus diver-

law in the concept of clerical immunity. Cocchi is content merely to present both views, and is satisfied with a rather generic explanation of the right of the Church to declare what is of divine law and to moderate clerical privileges.[28] Prümmer (†1931) presents a concise statement of the common view of the juridical origin of clerical immunity.[29] Chelodi rightly limits the scope of divine law in this matter to the *reasons* and *foundation* upon which clerical immunity is based.[30] Wernz-Vidal, whose treatise in this matter is limited to the privilege of the forum, rightly point out that the point at issue should be limited to the forum of clerics in temporal matters. They point out that although some of the reasons for the exemption of the clergy during the middle ages no longer exist, there are nevertheless sufficient reasons to warrant its substantial conservation, as condemned proposition 31 of the *Syllabus errorum* indicates.[31] These authors point out that the clergy below the Supreme Pontiff do not enjoy clerical immunity from strictly divine law. This refutes both of

sis temporibus prodiere, tamquam mere ecclesiasticae habendae sunt. Multa hic essent disputanda de varia anteactis aetatibus agendi ratione, hac in re ab Ecclesia adhibita."—*Ad codicem iuris canonici Benedicti XV Pont. Max. auctoritate promulgatum commentaria minora, comparativa methodo digesta concinnavit Doct. Albertus Toso* (Tiferni Tiberni, ex. offic. Typogr. Vinciana, 1921), ad. c. 120; cf. ad. c. 121.

[28] "Ecclesia vero ex nativa sua institutione, ius habet declarandi ius divinum et moderandi huiusmodi privilegia."—*Commentarius in codicem iuris canonici* (Taurini Augustinae: Marietti, 1922), lib. II, sect. I, pp. 73-74.

[29] "Hoc privilegium [fori] clericis et religiosis competit ex iure quidem humano, sed in iure divino fundamentum habet . . . Immunitas personalis clericorum [ab officiis et onere laicali] fundatur in ipsa ordinatione divina."—*Manuale iuris canonici* (5. ed., Friburgi Brisgoviae: Herder, 1927), pp. 86-87.

[30] "At ius divinum, si excipias R. Pontificem qui divina ordinatione nulli humani potestati subiectus est, non continet nisi rationes quae immunitatem expedire ostendunt, legem veterem quae eam statuerat nunc abrogatam, denique fundamentum cui innixa legitima auctoritas eam statuere potest."—*Ius de personis iuxta codicem iuris canonici* (2. ed., Trento: Libreria moderna di A. Ardesi & Co.), p. 191.

[31] *Ius canonicum ad codicis normam exactum* (7 toms. in 9 vols., Romae: apud aedes Universitatis Gregorianae, 1925-1938), vol. VI (1927), p. 45.

the hypotheses that had been adduced by Suarez. They point out, however, that in a broad and improper sense clerical exemption can be referred to divine law, in the sense already explained; and they clearly assign the proper efficient cause of clerical immunity to the dispositions of canon law.[32] Blat confines his treatment of the question to a strict commentary of the canons; and with regard to the juridical basis of immunity simply refers to the condemned propositions.[33] Augustine does not discuss the question of the juridical origin of clerical immunity in the latest edition of his commentary, although he refutes as a "pretension" the assertion that this privilege is of divine and natural law. His analysis is correct only with regard to the attribution of clerical immunity to natural and divine law *as its formal cause,* not in the sense explained according to the doctrine of canonists generally.[34]

Vermeersch-Creusen,[35] Lega (who explains that, since the

[32] "Clerici vero Rom. Pontifice inferiores exemptionem a foro saeculari nequaquam *ex stricto iure divino* consecuti sunt, quasi illa praerogativa singulis clericis immediate a Deo fuisset concessa, aut propter mandatum quoddam speciale Dei, Romano Pontifici datum, singuli clerici a foro saeculari essent eximendi. Verum ius divinum nonnisi sensu lato et improprie causa exemptionis clericorum dici potest, quatenus Rom. Pontifix vi sui officii convenienti quadam ratione pro diversitate temporum et locorum dignitati status clericalis consulere debet, et illa exemptio clerici in causis temporalibus aequitati naturali multum congruit. At *propria causa efficiens* huius exemptionis sunt leges *canonicae,* quibus immunitas illa clericorum aut immediate constituta et postea per leges quoque principum christianorum munita est, aut privilegia, quae per imperatores populosque christianos oblata Ecclesiae fuere ab ipsa accepta et pro sua potestate confirmata sunt."—*Ius canonicum ad codicis normam exactum,* VI, 46-47. This volume also contains a restatement of what appears to have been the original observation regarding derogation of the privileged forum by custom, which is here reproduced *supra,* p. 48, note 67. Cf. *Ius canonicum ad codicis normam exactum,* p. 48, note (85).

[33] "De iuridico fundamento huius immunitatis propp. 32 & 30."—*Commentarium textus codicis iuris canonici* (2 vols., Romae: F. Ferrari, 1931), lib. II, p. 72.

[34] *A commentary on the new code of canon law* vol. II, (6. ed., St. Louis: B. Herder Book Co., 1936), pp. 60-61, 65.

[35] "Immunitas quamquam in iure divino, sive naturali sive positivo,

time of Schmalzgrueber, this has become the common opinion)[36] and Roberti[37] not only conform to the common opinion, but employ the very terminology that is suggested by the authors in public law.[38]

With the single exception of Augustine the authors can be said to be in substantial agreement regarding the juridical origin of clerical immunity.

Article 3. Evaluation of the Common Opinion

It must be remembered that the reason for clerical immunity is the reverence and respect which is due to persons who are especially dedicated to the service of God. This reverence and respect is due to the clergy in view of their sacred character. To this extent, at least, and apart from its determinations and applications, clerical immunity can be said to be of divine law. Writers of the nineteenth and twentieth centuries recognize this just as clearly as did those of the seventeenth and eighteenth. In substance, therefore, they are not in disagreement with the older authors. It can be observed, however, that nearly all the older authors posited some *obligation,* although they granted that it was not an obligation in justice, to observe clerical immunity. Although the majority of these writers admitted that divine law was not the formal cause of clerical immunity, nevertheless, they

fundamentum habet, proxime et *formaliter* ex lege tantum Ecclesiae oritur."—*Epitome iuris canonici* (5-6. ed., 3 vols., Mechliniae-Romae: H. Dessain), vol. I (6. ed., 1937), 214.

[36] *Commentarius in iudicia ecclesiastica* (2 vols., Romae: Anonima Libraria Cattolica Italiana), vol. I (1938), 82-83.

[37] "Alii denique mediam viam secuti docuerunt privilegium immediate ex iure humano, fundamentaliter ex iure divino profluere. Arguunt ex oppositis argumentis praecedentium sententiarum et ex Tridentino quod supponit introductum fuisse divina ordinatione et canonicis sanctionibus.

"Substantialiter huic sententiae adhaeremus, dicentes privilegium esse iuris humani sed maxime clericis convenire, qui cum laicis praeesse debeant, nequeunt ab ipsis iudicari."—*De processibus* (2. ed., Romae: Marietti, 1940), pp. 142-143.

[38] Cappello, *Summa iuris publici ecclesiastici,* p. 458; Coronata, *Ius publicum ecclesiasticum,* p. 209; Ottaviani, *Institutiones iuris publici ecclesiastici,* I, 406; Cavagnis, *Institutiones iuris publici ecclesiastici,* I, 184.

seem to convey the impression that civil law and canon law were in some way already bound by the natural law to concede clerical exemption. Modern writers do not see any such obligation with regard to those things which are not native rights of the Church and hence formally of divine law.[39] Moreover, the controversy over the precise title by which civil laws bind the clergy is now settled. Such laws can be said to oblige *vi legis* unless they are contrary to divine or ecclesiastical law. This has helped to clarify the position of Catholic writers in their view of clerical immunity.

The examination of the arguments advanced in favor of the opinion that there is some element of divine law in clerical immunity reveals substantially what the majority of the older authors admitted, namely that they do not establish the existence of a proper formal precept of natural or divine positive law in regard to clerical immunity in the stricter or more restricted sense. Coronata rightly observes that the opinion which would see a formal precept of divine law in this matter at least as proposed by Reiffenstuel and Ferraris, does not clearly observe the distinction between immunities properly so called and native rights which are proper to the Church as a perfect society independent of the State. His own specific contribution is the suggestion that this distinction be observed in order that any apparent dissension in terminology may be avoided. Cappello, too, expresses this desire.[40] Ottaviani does not substantially disagree with this proposition. He points out *first* that no single exclusive theory can be proposed regarding the juridical cause of all immunities; inasmuch as some are formally of civil law, others are of divine law, others at least in their specific determination are of ecclesiastical law. Again, Ottaviani observes *secondly* that some things are native rights rather than immunities; that is they are determinations or immediate consequences of rights which flow from the native constitution of the Church as a perfect society independent of the State. *Thirdly,* he states that in matters outside this category, clerical immunity is of divine law basically; in view of

39 Cf. Coronata, *Ius publicum ecclesiasticum,* p. 193.

40 Coronata, *Ius publicum ecclesiasticum,* pp. 210-211; Cappello, *Summa iuris publici ecclesiastici,* p. 458.

the religious dignity that is inherent in sacred persons, and inasmuch as the Church by the divine power committed to her can vindicate these exemptions.[41]

This is what the arguments developed throughout the course of this dissertation established. This explains how the Church could make changes in the discipline of clerical immunity and retain this juridical institution in substance. This native right explains how the Church exercises her proper authority and does not usurp that of the State; for the Church is the judge of the congruity of the obligations which civil laws impose, with the dignity and reverence of the clerical state. By virtue of her indirect power in temporal matters, the Church can withdraw sacred presons from such obligations, or in other words, constitute their exemption.

Coronata clearly warns his readers that his proposed "clearer statement of the question" and limitation of the concept of clerical immunity to those exemptions which are not native rights that pertain to the very essence of the Church or necessarily flow from her juridical independence, is in no sense to be regarded as a new theory; it is simply a means to facilitate the solution of the problem according to the common view of Catholic authors.[42]

The quotations from the authors cited in the preceding article indicate that this fully univocal notion of clerical immunity in the strict sense is lacking; that in regard to the immunities in the strict sense as distinguished from native rights, there is substantial agreement; and that the observation that clerical immunity is formally of ecclesiastical law but basically and remotely of divine law is the common and true opinion.[43]

The matter developed throughout the pages of this essay can be synopsised in the following manner:

[41] *Institutiones iuris publici ecclesiastici,* I, 405.

[42] *Ius publicum ecclesiasticum,* p. 215.

[43] Coronata, *Ius publicum ecclesiasticum,* p. 209; Lega, *Commentarius in iudicia ecclesiastica,* I, 32; Ottaviani *Institutiones iuris publici ecclesiastici,* I, 406; Cappello, *Summa iuris publici ecclesiastici,* p. 458; Cavagnis, *Institutiones iuris publici ecclesiastici,* II, 184; and other authors cited in preceding article.

I. *Clerical immunity is not formally of divine law.* Divine law does not establish each and every particular clerical exemption. That which divine law establishes and determines is not an immunity properly so called, but rather a native right. The divine law whereby the Church can establish clerical exemption is an example of this native right, but is not in itself a clerical immunity.

II. *Clerical immunity proceeds formally from ecclesiastical or civil law.* If clerical immunity were formally of divine law, civil laws contrary to it would be *ipso facto* invalid. Clerical immunity, on the contrary, implies the concept of an exemption from a valid civil law whose obligation would be binding upon the clergy, had the Church not decreed their exemption from it.

III. *Clerical immunity is basically and fundamentally of divine law.* The Church proceeds directly or indirectly by virtue of her superiority over the State; directly, in regard to strictly spiritual matters and indirectly in regard to immunities strictly called. Thus she may grant immunities herself (withdraw the clergy from the obligation to observe certain civil laws), or she may ratify and *canonize* such civil laws as grant the exemption. Moreover, in the sense explained above, in view of the great congruity of clerical immunity with divine law, and the examples and testimonies of Sacred Scripture, this institution can be called fundamentally, basically and remotely of divine law.

These three propositions represent an analysis of the common view regarding the juridical nature of clerical immunity. Its proof may be stated thus: the opinion regarding its juridical nature is to be admitted which is best in keeping with the nature of clerical immunity; which best explains the changes in ecclesiastical discipline regarding this institution; and which is in agreement with the statements of the *magisterium* of the Church.

I. *The common opinion is best in keeping with the nature of clerical immunity.* Clerical immunity is an exemption, not from any law, but from a valid law. The Church, whose right it is, decides that the obligations which this law imposes commonly on citizens, are incongruous with the reverence and dignity of the clerical state. This action by the Church is made by virtue of power divinely conferred upon her, in view of the supernatural purpose of the clerical state, and in accordance with examples and testimonies of Holy Writ.

II. *The common opinion best explains the history of clerical immunity.* The evidence of history shows that immunities are not merely concessions of civil law; the action of the Holy See, especially during and after the eleventh century reform movement brings into bold relief the incongruity of the subjection of the ecclesiastical to the lay power. Nor is evidence lacking regarding the firm stand taken by the popes and councils from the fourth and fifth centuries. The suitability of clerical exemption can vary according to different circumstances of place and time. Whence it can be easily understood how the Church could be more severe at certain times, and more relaxed in her discipline at other times, if it is admitted that the immunities are formally of ecclesiastical law.

III. *The common opinion is completely in conformity with the* statements of the *magisterium* of the Church. These documents explicitly reprobate the theory of the Protestants, regalists and liberals that clerical immunity is of civil law. They positively establish that *clerical immunity is not only of human law, but of divine law as well; that it was constituted by the ordinance of God and canonical sanctions.* These expressions do not necessarily indicate that clerical immunity is formally of divine law; they are sufficiently explained by the proposition that clerical immunity is *basically, fundamentally* and *remotely* of divine law, and *proximately, immediately* and *formally* of ecclesiastical law. Nor can it be proved that the mind of the Church has been to define that some immunities are formally of divine law, and that others are of human law; for the canonical documents refer to immunity in general, without distinction, and attribute this institution to divine as well as to human law. Coronata implies that they exclude from the notion of immunities those rights which formally accrue to the Church formally from divine law and which are native rights rather than immunities in the strict sense.[44]

[44] *Ius publicum ecclesiasticum,* p. 215.

CONCLUSIONS

I. The differences among Catholic writers regarding the juridical origin of clerical immunity have been mainly verbal, and have been due to the lack of a clear distinction between native rights and immunities in the strict sense. Nevertheless, the older writers were more prone to postulate some obligation according to th natural law, although not an obligation in justice. Present-day writers posit no such obligation on the part of the State prior to an ecclesiastical decree on this matter.

II. Between the fourth and the twelfth century the popes proclaimed the principle: *Ecclesia iudicat de fide et sacerdotibus.* Especially during the reform movement of Gregory VII there was a clarification of the principle that the laity have no jurisdiction over the clergy; but as yet the civil law did not recognize the concept of a complete exemption of the clergy from the secular power. This was the period prior to the full guaranty of the total exemption of the clergy and their goods in civil as well as ecclesiastical legislation.

III. From the III general Council of the Lateran (1179) to the law of the concordats in the eighteenth and nineteenth centuries, aside from such special concessions as may have been made by the Holy See to individual kings, the ecclesiastical legislation indicates that the concept of clerical immunity involved a complete lack of jurisdiction on the part of the civil power over the persons or over the goods of ecclesiastics.

IV. In the legislation of the eighteenth and nineteenth centuries and in the Code, the idea of a complete exemption of the clergy from civil authority is not essential to the concept of clerical immunity.

V. Clerical immunities in their juridical origin are formally of ecclesiastical law; however they have a basis or foundation in divine law. This basis is twofold: the right of the Church to decree the exemption of the clergy from such civil obligations as are incompatible either in whole or in part with the reverence and dignity due to the clerical state, and the supernatural motives upon which this exemption is based.

VI. The opinion that clerical immuunity in its origin, essence and abolition exists by the mere *fiat* of the civil power is untenable. It contradicts the right of the Church to exempt her clergy from civil laws that are incompatible with their sacred functions and obligations; and, it implies that the Church is not indirectly superior to the State by reason of her higher purpose or end.

VII. The Holy See derogates from clerical immunity in view of particular circumstances by privileges and concordats. However it does not and cannot abolish clerical immunity to the extent that there would be no distinction whatever before the civil law between the clergy and the laity.

VIII. Custom, within proper limits, can now be admitted even though it may be somewhat derogatory to clerical immunity. It cannot bring about the total abolition of clerical immunity. Thus no custom can abolish the ecclesiastical forum in the sense of canon 1553, § 1, 3°, although the Holy See has admitted the force of custom in Germany and Belgium against what are now some of the provisions of canon 120. This does not imply, however, that the permission necessary to convene the clergy in civil courts can be neglected on the plea of contrary custom. At all events, the ordinary should be advised regarding the proceeding.

IX. The dictum of Cardinal Bellarmine that "the canonists asserted what the theologians did not deny" is the key to the explanation of the variant views regarding the juridical origin of clerical immunity.

X. The controversy over the precise title by which civil law obliges the clergy is now solved: these laws bind *vi legis* unless they be contrary to divine law or to an exemption rightly established by the Church.

BIBLIOGRAPHY

Sources

Acta Apostolicae Sedis, Commentarium Officiale, Romae, 1909—

Acta Sanctae Sedis, 41 vols., Romae, 1865-1908.

Acta Pontificum Romanorum Inedita, ed. a J. von Pflugh-Hartung, 3 vols., Tübingen, 1881-1886.

Bruns, Hermanus, *Canones Apostolorum et Conciliorum Saeculorum IV, V, VI, VII,* 2 vols., Berolini, 1839.

Bullarium Diplomatum et Privilegiorum Sanctorum Romanorum Ponticum Taurinensis editio, ed. a Francisco Gaudé, 24 vols. + appendix, Augustae Taurinorum, 1857-1872.

Canones et Decreta Sacrosancti Oecumenici Concilii Tridentini, [ ] ed., Romae, 1845.

Capitularia Regum Francorum, Monumenta Germaniae Historica legum sectio I, 5 toms., edd. A. Boretius & V. Krause, Hannoverae, 1897.

Codex Iuris Canonici Pii X Pontificis Maximi iussu digestus Benedicti Papae XV auctoritate promulgatus, Romae, 1918.

Codex Theodosianus cum Perpetuis Commentariis Iacobi Gothofredi, ed. Antonius Marvilus, 2. ed., 6 vols., Lipsiae, 1740.

Codicis Iuris Canonici Fontes cura Emi. Card. Gasparri editi, 9 vols., Romae [later, Civitate Vaticana]: Typis Polyglottis Vaticanis, 1923-1939. Vols. VII-IX ed. cura et studio Emi. Justiniani Card. Serédi.

Codicis Iuris Canonici Schemata, lib. IV, de processibus, pars I *de iudiciis in genere* digessit Franciscus Roberti, Civitate Vaticana: Pontificium institutum utriusque iuris, 1940.

Collectio Judiciorum de Novis Erroribus, qui ab initio duodecimi saeculi usque ad annum 1632 *in Ecclesia proscripti sunt et notati,* a Carolo Du Plessis D'Argentere, 2 toms., Lutetiae Parisiorum, 1728.

Constitutiones et Acta Publica Imperatorum et Regum, Monumenta Germaniae Historica legum sectio IV, 8 toms., (t. II ed. L. Weiland, Hannoverae, 1896).

Corpus Iuris Canonici, Editio Lipsiensis post Iusti Henningii Bohmeri curas . . . denuo edidit Aemilius Ludovicus Richter, 2 vols., Lipsiae 1839.

Corpus Iuris Civilis, edd. P. Krueger, T. Mommsen, R. Schoell, G. Kroll, 5 (15) ed., 3 vols., Berolini: Apud Weidmannos, 1928.

Decretales D. Gregorii Papae IX suae integritati una cum glossis restituta, [ ] ed., 2 vols., Romae, 1582.

Decretum Gratiani emendatum et notationibus illustratum una cum glossis, [ ] ed., 2 vols., Romae, 1632.

Enchiridion Symbolorum Definitionum et Declarationum de Rebus Fidei et Morum, edd. H. Denzinger, C. Bannwart, J. Umberg, 21.-23. ed., Friburgi Brisgoviae: Herder & Co., 1937.

Gregorii I Papae Registrum Epistolarum, Monumenta Germaniae Historica Epistolarum sectio II, 7 toms. (t. I in 2 parts), edd. P. Ewald & M. Hartmann, Hannoverae, 1887-1928.

Haenel, G., *Lex Romana Visigothorum,* 3 ed., post Sichardum, Lipsiae, 1849.

Harduin, Jean, *Acta Conciliorum et Epistolae Decretales ac Constitutiones Summorum Pontificum,* 12 vols., Parisiis, 1715.

Mansi, Joannes D., *Sacrorum Conciliorum Nova et Amplissima Collectio,* 53 vols., Parisiis, Arnhem, Lipsiae, 1901-1927.

Mercati, *Raccolta di Concordati su Materie Ecclesiastiche tra la Santa Sede e l'Authorità Civili,* Roma: Tipografia Poliglotta Vaticana, 1919.

Migne, J. P., *Patrologiae Cursus Completus, Series Graeca,* 161 vols., Parisiis, 1857-1866.

———, *Patrologiae Cursus Completus, Series Latina,* 221 vols., Parisiis, 1844-1855.

Nussi, V., *Conventiones de Rebus Ecclesiasticis inter S. Sedem et Civilem Potestatem variis formis initae ex Collectione Romana Excerptae,* Moguntiae, 1870.

Perugini, Angelus, *Concordata Vigentia Notis Historicis et Indiciis Declarata,* Romae: apud custodiam librariam Pont. Instituti Utriusque Iuris, 1934.

Roskovány, Augustin, *Monumenta Catholica pro Independentia Potestatis Ecclesiasticae ab Imperio Civili,* 13 vols., Quinque Ecclesiis [Fünfkirchen] et Nitriae, 1847-1879.

Theodosiani Libri XVI cum Constitutionibus Sirmondianis et Leges Novellae ad Theodosianum Pertinentes, edd. T. Mommsen & P. Meyer, 3 vols., Berolini, 1905.

Thiel, Andreas, *Epistolae Romanorum Pontificum Genuinae a S. Hilario ad Pelagium II,* Brunsbergae, 1868.

Authors

[Anonymous], *De Finibus Utriusque Potestatis Ecclesiasticae et Laicae,* auctore D * * * *, Lugani et Ratisbonae, 1781.

———, *Synopsis Pirhingiana,* [ ] ed., Romae, 1849.

Aichner, Simon, *Compendium Juris Ecclesiastici,* 6. ed., Brixiae, 1887.

Albers, P., *Enchiridion Historiae Ecclesiasticae Universae,* 3. ed., 3 vols., Neomagii in Hollandia, 1910.

Alteserra, Antonius, *Opera Omnia,* 1. ed. Neopolitana, II toms., Neapoli, 1777.

Ambrosio, D., *Commentaria in Bullam Gregorii XIV de Immunitate et Libertate Ecclesiastica,* 4. ed., Bracciani, 1633.

Antonelli, Joannes, *Tractatus Posthumus de Juribus et Oneribus Clericorum in duos libros distributus,* Romae, 1699.

Azorius Lorcitano, I., *Institutionum Moralium Pars Prima,* [ ] ed., Brixiae, 1617.

[Bachofen], Charles Augustine, *A Commentary on the New Code of Canon Law,* 6. ed., St. Louis: B. Herder Book Co., 1936.

Badii, Caesar, *Institutiones Iuris Canonici,* 3. ed., Florentiae: Libreria Editrice Florentina, 1921.

Barbosa, Augustinus, *Iuris Ecclesiastici Universi libri tres,* [ ] ed., Lugduni, 1659.

Bellarminus, Robertus, *Disputationum Roberti Bellarmini de Controversiis Christianae Fidei,* 7 vols., vol. II, *de clericis,* [ ] ed., Venetiis, 1721.

Benedictus XIV, *De Synodo Dioecesana libri* 13 *in duos tomos,* [ ] ed., Venetiis, 1792.

Berardi, Carolus, *Gratiani Canones Genuinae ab Apocryphis Discreti,* 4 toms., Venetiis, 1777.

Bianchi, G. Antonio di Lucca, *Della Potesta e della Politia Chiesa,* 3 toms., Roma, 1745.

Blat, Albertus, *Commentarium Textus Codicis Iuris Canonici,* 2. ed., 2 vols., Romae: F. Ferrari, 1931.

Böchn, Placidus, *Commentarius in Jus Canonicum Umiversum sive in Quinque Libros Decretalium Gregorii IX Pont. Max.,* 3 toms., Salisburgi, 1776.

Böhmer, Iustus, *Ius Ecclesiasticum Protestanticum Iuris Canonici iuxta seriem Decretalium Ostendens,* 5. ed., 5 toms. in 4, Haale Magdenburgiae, 1746.

Boyd, William K., *The Ecclesiastical Edicts of the Theodosian Code,* Studies in History, Economics and Public Law, edited by the Faculty of Political Science of Columbia University, vol. XXIV, n. 2, New York: The Columbia University Press, 1905.

Bozio Eugubino, T., *De Iure Status sive de Iure Divino et Naturali Ecclesiasticae Libertatis ed Potestatis,* Romae, 1600.

Buckland, W., *A Manual of Roman Private Law,* Cambridge: The University Press, 1923.

Calvinus, Joannes, *Institutionum Christianae Religionis Libri Quattor,* [ ] ed., Amstelodami, 1667.

Cappello, Felix M., *Institutiones Iuris Publici Ecclesiastici,* 2 vols., Augustae Taurinorum, 1907.

———, *Summa Iuris Publici Ecclesiastici,* Romae, apud Aedes Universitatis Gregorianae, 1928.

Catholic Encyclopedia, The, 15 vols. and 2 supplements, New York, 1907-1922.

Cavagnis, Felix M., *Institutiones Iuris Publici Ecclesiastici,* 3 ed., 3 vols., Romae, 1883.

Chelodi, Ioannes, *Ius de Personis iuxta Codicem Iuris Canonici,* 2. ed., Tridenti: Libreria moderna di A. Ardesi & Co., 1927.

Cicognani, Amleto, *Canon Law,* 2. ed., authorized English version, revised by J. O'Hara and F. Brennan, Philadelphia: Dolphin Press, 1935.

Cocchi, G., *Commentarius in Codicem Iuris Canonici,* lib. II, pars I, Taurinorum Augustae: Marietti, 1922.

Coronata, Matthaeus Conte a, *Ius Publicum Ecclesiasticum,* 2. ed., Taurini: Marietti, 1934.

Covarruvias, Didacus, *Opera Omnia,* 2 vols., [ ] ed., Coloniae Allobrogum, 1679.

De Angelis, Philippus, *Praelectiones Iuris Canonici ad Methodum Decretalium Gregorii IX Exactae,* [ ] ed., 5 vols., Romae, 1879.

Decius, *Philippi Decii Mediolanensis in Decretales Commentaria necnon in Titulum de Privilegiis,* Lugani, 1576.

De Francisci, Pietro, *Per la Storia dell' Episcopalis Audientiá,* Roma, 1915.

De Lacombe, C., *Recueil de Jurisprudence Canonique et Beneficiale par Ordre Alphabetique,* 2. ed., Paris, 1771.

De Lugo, Ioannes, *Disputationum de Iustitia et Iure Tomus Secundus,* [ ] ed., Lugduni, 1680.

De Marca, Petrus, *Dissertationum de Concordia Sacerdotii et Imperii seu de Libertatibus Ecclesiae Gallicanae Libri Octo,* 3. ed., Parisiis, 1771.

De Meester, Alphonsus, *Juris Canonici et Juris Canonico-Civilis Compendium,* 2. ed., 3 vols., Brugis: Descleé de Brouwer et S., 1923-1928.

De Oliva, Felicianus, *Tractatus de Foro Ecclesiae,* Coloniae Allobrogum, 1733.

Diana, Antonius, *R. P. D. Antonii Diana Panormitani Clerici Regularis Resolutiones Morales in Tres Partes Distributae,* 3. ed., Lugduni, 1635.

Dreidon, Joannes, *Joannis Dreidonis a Turnhout de Libertate Christiana Liber* Lovanii, 1540.

Duardus, L., *Commentaria in Bullam S. D. N. D. Pauli Quinti Lectam in Die Coenae Domini MDCXVIII in Tres Libros Distincta, Mediolani,* 1620.

Fagnanus, Prosperus, *Ius Canonicum seu Commentaria Absolutissima in Quinque Decretalium Libros,* [ ] ed., 3 vols., Venetiis, 1729.

Fatolillus, Joannes B., *Theatrum Immunitatis et Libertatis Ecclesiasticae,* 2 vols., Romae, 1714.

Ferraris, F. Lucius, *Prompta Biblotheca Canonica Iuridica Moralis Theologica necnon Ascetica Polemica Rubricistica Historica,* [ ] ed., 9 vols., Romae, 1885-1899.

Ferreres, Ioannes Baptista, *Institutiones Canonicae iuxta Novissimum Codicem Pii X,* 2. ed., 2 vols., Romae, 1920.

Garcia, Juan de la Cruz, *La Seudo-Defensa quae el Senor Vigil Hace de los Gobiernos Refutada por si Miasma,* Lima, 1866.

Gignac, Josephus, *Compendium Juris Canonici de Personis,* Quebec, 1901.

Gonzalez-Tellez, Emmanuel, *Commentaria Perpeua in Singulos Textus Quinque Librorum Decretalium Gregorii IX,* [ ] ed., 5 vols., Venetiis, 1756.

Govarts, Petrus, *Certamen Immunitatis Sacerdotum Belgii in Causis Personalibus praecipue Criminalibus,* [Mechliniae, 1720 ?]

Grandclaude, Eugenius, *Jus Canonicum juxta Ordinem Decretalium,* 5 toms. in 4, Parisiis, 1882.

Hefele, C., and Le Clercq, H., *Histoire des Conciles d'apres les Documents Originaux,* 10 vols. in 19, Paris, 1907-1938.

Heiner, Franciscus, *De Processu Criminali Ecclesiastico,* ed. A. Wynen, Romae, 1912.

Hergenröther, Joseph, *Catholic Church and Christian State,* 2 vols., in 1, London, 1876.

Hostiensis, [Henricus de Segusio], *Henrici Cardinalis Hostiensis Summa Aurea,* Lugduni, 1568.

———, *In Quinque Decretalium Libros Commentaria,* Venetiis, 1581.

Hull, Robert, *Medieval Theories of the Papacy and Other Essays,* collected and arranged by Edmund F. Sutcliffe, London: Burns, Oates and Washbourne, Ltd., 1934.

Jolowitz, H. F., *Historical Introduction to the Study of Roman Law,* Cambridge: The University Press, 1932.

Laux, J., *Church History,* New York: Benziger Brothers, 1935.

Laymann, Paulus, *Theologiae Moralis in Quinque Libros Positae,* 5 toms., Venetiis, 1719.

Lega, Michael, *Commentarius in Iudicia Ecclesiatica iuxta Codicem Iuris Canonici,* 2 vols., Romae: Anonima Libraria Cattolica Italiana, 1938.

Lessius, Leonardus, *De Iustitia et Iure Libri Quattor,* 3. ed., Antverpiae, 1612.

Leurenius, P., *Forum Ecclesiasticum, in quo Ius Canonicum Universum Librorum ac Titulorum Ordine Decretalium Explanatur,* Moguntiae, 1717-1735.

Liberatore, Mathieu, *Le Droit Public de l'Eglise,* tr. & ed., A. Onclair, Paris, 1888.

Makeé, Ch., *Institutiones Juris Ecclesiastici tum Publici tum Privati,* 2 toms., Parisiis, 1897.

Maroto, Philippus, *Institutiones Iuris Canonici ad Norman Novi Codicis,* 3. ed., 2 vols., Romae: Apud Commentarium pro Religiosis, 1921.

Marsilius Pataviensis, *The Defensor Pacis of Marsilius of Padua edited by C. W. Previté-Orton,* Cambridge: The University Press, 1928.

Maschat a S. Erasmo, Remigius, *Institutiones Canonicae,* 2 toms., Romae, 1751.

Medina, Bartholomeus, *Expositio in Primam Secundae Angelici Doctoris D. Thomae Aquinatis,* 3. ed., Venetiis, 1590.

Medina, Ioannes, *Ioannis Medinae de Poenitentia, Restitutione et Contractibus Praeclarum et Absolutum Opus in Duos divisum Tomos,* 2 toms., in 1 vol., Inglostadii, 1581.

Molina, Ludovicus, *Ludovici Molinae de Iustitia et Iure Tomus Primus de Contractibus,* Moguntiae, 1609.

Navarrus [Martinus de Azpilcueta], *Martini ab Azpilcueta Doctoris Navarri Consiliorum sive Responsionum Libri Quinque iuxta Ordinem Decretalium Dispositi,* 3. ed., 2 toms., Romae, 1620.

———, *Opera Omnia in Sex Tomos Distributa,* [ ] ed., Venetiis, 1618.

Ojetti, Benedictus, *Synopsis Rerum Moralium et Iuris Pontificii,* Romae, 1899.

Ottaviani, Alaphridus, *Institutiones Iuris Publici Ecclesiastici,* 2. ed., 2 vols., Civitate Vaticana: Typis Polyglottis Vaticanis, 1935-1936.

Panormitanus [Nicholas de Tudeschis], *Nicolai Tudeschii Catinensis Siculi Panormitani Archiepiscopi vulgo Abbatis Panormitani Omnia quae extant Commentaria in Decretalium Libros,* 10 toms., Venetiis, 1588.

———, *Reportorium Antonii Corseti Siculi ad Nicolai Abbatis Panormitani Commentaria super Decretalium et Clementinam Libros,* Venetiis, 1777.

Pehem, Josephus Joannes Nepomoucene, *Praelectionum in Jus Ecclesiasticum Pars. I, comprehendens Jus Ecclesiasticum Publicum,* Viennae, 1785.

Pichler, Vitus, *Epitome Juris Canonici juxta Decretalium Libros Gregorianae Collectionis Explanati,* [ ] ed., 2 vols., Venetiis, 1765.

Pirhing, Ernricus, *Jus Canonicum in V Libros Decretalium Distributum* [ ] ed., Dillingae, 1774.

Prümmer, Dominicus, *Manuale Iuris Canonici,* 5. ed., Friburgi Brisgoviae: Herder & Co., 1927.

Reiffenstuel, Anacletus, *Ius Canonicum Universum,* 5 vols. in 7, [ ] ed., Monachii, 1702.

Roberti, Franciscus, *De Processibus,* 2. ed., Romae: apud Aedes Facultatis Iuridicae ad D. Apollinaris, 1940.

Sanguinetti, Sebastianus, *Iuris Ecclesiastici Privati Institutiones,* Romae, 1884.

Santi, Franciscus, *Praelectiones Juris Canonici juxta Ordinem Decretalium Gregorii IX,* [ ] ed., 2 vols., Ratisbonae, Neo-Eboraci, Cincinnatii, 1892.

Sartolli, Franciscus, *Prima Principia Iuris Publici Ecclesiastici de Concordatis,* Romae, 1888.

Schmalzgrueber, Franciscus, *Ius Ecclesiasticum Universum,* [ ] ed., 5 vols. in 12, Romae, 1842-1845.

Soglia, Joannes, *Institutiones Iuris Publici Ecclesiastici,* 5. ed., Paris [sic], 1853.

Soto, Dominicus, *Dominici Soto Segobiensis in Quartum (quam vocant) Sententiarum Tomus Secundus,* [ ] ed., Venetiis, 1575.

Squillante, P. *Tractatus de Privilegiis Clericorum,* 3. ed., Neapoli, 1635.

Suarezius, Franciscus, *R. P. Francisci Suarezii Opera Omnia,* 26 vols., Bruxellis et Parisiis: apud Ludovicum Vivés, 1856-1861, tom. XXIV (1859), *Opuscula sex inedita,* instruxit Joannes Baptista Mallon, lib. II, *de Immunitate Ecclesiastica a Venetis Violata;* tom. XXV (1859), *Defensio Catholicae Fidei adversus Anglicanae Sectae Errores,* ed. a Carolo Berton, lib. IV, *de Immunitate Ecclesiastica seu Exemptione Clericorum a Jurisdictione Temporalium Principum.*

Sturzo, Luigi, *Church and State,* New York: Longmans, Green & Co., 1939.

Thomas Aquinas, *Doctoris Angelici Divi Thomae Aquinatis Opera Omnia,* 34 vols., Parisiis: apud Ludovicum Vivès, 1871-1882. Vol. XX (1876), *Commentarium ad Epist. ad Romanos,* 565.

Toso, Albertus, *Ad Codicem Iuris Canonici Benedicti XV Pont. Max. auctoritate promulgatum Commentaria Minora Comparativo Methodo Digesta concinnavit Doct. Albertus Toso,* lib. II, Tiferni Tiberini: ex officina Typogr. Vinciana, 1921.

Van Espen, Zegerus Bernardus, *Jus Ecclesiasticum Universum seu Commentaria in Canones Juris Veteris ac Novi et in Jus Novissimum, Opus Posthumum,* [ ] ed., 5 vols., Lovanii et Lugduni, 1853-1868.

Van Hove, Alphonsus, *Prolegomena ad Codicem Iuris Canonici—Commentarium Lovaniense in Codicem Iuris Canonici,* vol. I, tom. I, Mechliniae-Romae: H. Dessain, 1928.

Vecchiotti, Septimus, *Institutiones Canonicae,* 19. ed., 3 vols., Augustae-Taurinorum, 1886.

Vermeersch, Authurus, et Creusen, Iosephus, *Epitome Iuris Canonici,* 3 vols., (vol. I, 6. ed., 1937; vol. II, 5. ed., 1936; vol. III, 5. ed., 1934), Mechliniae-Romae: H. Dessain.

Vermigli, Petrus Martire, *Loci Communes Petri Martyris Vermilii Florentini,* [ ] ed., Genevae, 1626.

Vigil, Francesco de Paula Gonzalez, *Defensa de la Authoridad de los Gobiernos y de los Obispos contra las Pretenciones de la Curia Romana,* 2. ed., 6 toms. in 3 vols., Lima, 1848.

Wernz, Franciscus X., *Ius Decretalium,* 2. ed., 6 vols., Romae et Prati, 1896-1912.

Wernz, Franciscus X., et Vidal, Petrus, *Ius Canonicum ad Codicis Normam Exactum,* 7 toms. in 9 vols., Romae: apud Aedes Universitatis Gregorianae, 1923-1938.

Zallinger, Jacobus, *Institutiones Juris Ecclesiastici maxime Privati Ordine Decretalium,* [ ] ed., 5 vols., Romae, 1823.

Periodicals

American Ecclesiastical Review, The, (later *The Ecclesiastical Review*), Philadelphia, 1889—

Arkiv für katholisches Kirchenrecht, Innsbruck, 1857-1861; Mainz, 1862—

Jurist, The, Published by the School of Canon Law: The Catholic University of America, Washington, 1941—

Periodica de Re Canonica et Morali utili Praesertim Religiosis et Missionariis, Brugis, 1905—

Principle Articles

Ayrinhac, H., "The Motu Proprio 'Quantavis diligentia'," *AER,* XLVII (1912), 303-318.

———, "Clerics and Secular Tribunals," *AER,* XLVI (1911), 175-179.

Grashof, Otto, "Die Gesetze der römischen Kaiser über die Immunitäten des Klerus," *AKKR,* XXXVII (1877), 256-293.

———, "Die Annerkennung des privilegirten Gerichsstands des Klerus durch die römischen Kaiser," *AKKR,* XXXVIII (1877), 3-29.

Heiner, Franz, "Das Motuproprio 'Quantavis diligentia' Pius' X v. 9 Oktober 1911 und die deutsche 'Rechtsstaat'," *AKKR,* XCII (1912), 270-295.

Kuttner, Stephan, "The Father of The Science of Canon Law," *The Jurist,* I (1941), 3.

"Quirinus" [sic], "The Catholic Clergy in Politics," *AER,* XII (1895), 44-50 & 218-226.

Vermeersch, Arthurus, [Comment on "Quantavis diligentia,' n. 538; cf. n. 563] *Periodica,* VI (1912), 106-109; cf. 190.

Abbreviations

Acta Conciliorum—Harduin, *Acta Conciliorum et Epistolae Decretales ac Constituitones Summorum Pontificum*

AER—*American Ecclesiastical Review*

AKKR—*Arkiv für katholisches Kirchenrecht*

C—*Codex* (*Justinianus*)

C. Th.—*Codex Theodosianus*

Canones—Bruns, *Canones Apostolorum et Conciliorum Saeculorum IV-VII*

Collectio Judiciorum—Carolus Du Plessis D'Argentere, *Collectio Judiciorum—de Novis Erroribus, etc.*

Conventiones—Nussi, *Conventiones de Rebus Ecclesiasticis*, etc.

D—*Digest*

de Clericis—Bellarminus, *Disputationum Roberti Belarmini de Controversiis Christianae Fidei vol. II, de Clericis*

de Immunitate Ecclesiastica—Suarezius, *R. P. Francisci Suarezii Opera Omnia*, tom. XXV, lib. IV, *de Immunitate Ecclesiastica seu Exemptione Clericorum a Jurisdictione Temporalium Principum.*

Enchiridion—Albers, *Enchiridion Historiae Ecclesiasticae Universae*

Enchiridion Symbolorum—Denzinger, *Enchiridion Symbolorum, Definitionum*, etc.

Fontes—*Codicis Iuris Canonici Fontes*

Mansi—Mansi, *Sacrorum Conciliorum Nova et Amplissima Collectio*

MGH—*Monumenta Germaniae Historica*

MPG—Migne, *Patrologiae Cursus Completus, Series Graeca*

MPL—Migne, *Patrologiae Çursus Completus, Series Latina*

N—*Novellae*

Periodica—*Periodica de Re Canonica et Morali*

Prolegomena, Van Hove, *Prolegomena ad Codicem Iuris Canonici*

Roskovány, *Monumenta Catholica*—Roskovány, *Monumenta Catholica pro Potestatis Ecclesiasticae ab Imperio Civili*

BIOGRAPHICAL NOTE

John Emmanual Downs was born in the Bronx, New York City, N. Y., December 23, 1910. He attended St. Brendan's Parochial School and Cathedral College—the preparatory seminary of the Archdiocese of New York—in New York City, from which institution he received the degree of Bachelor of Arts. In 1929 he entered St. Joseph's Seminary of the Archdiocese of New York, and was ordained to the Priesthood on June 7, 1935. Father Downs served for two years as an assistant at the Church of the Magdalene, Pocantico Hills, New York; and for a year and a half at the American National Shrine of St. Ann, in New York City. In 1938 he entered the School of Canon Law at the Catholic University of America, from which institution he received the Baccalaureate in Canon Law in June 1939. In the same month of the following year he received the Licentiate in Canon Law.

INDEX

CANON LAW STUDIES

1. Freriks, Rev. Celestine A., C.PP.S., J.C.D., Religious Congregations in Their External Relations, 121 pp., 1916.
2. Galliher, Rev. Daniel M., O.P., J.C.D., Canonical Elections, 117 pp., 1917.
3. Borkowski, Rev. Aurelius L., O.F.M., J.C.D., De Confraternitatibus Ecclesiasticis, 136 pp., 1918.
4. Castillo, Rev. Cayo, J.C.D., Disertacion Historico-Canonica sobre la Potestad del Cabildo en Sede Vacante o Impedida del Vicario Capitular, 99 pp., 1919 (1918).
5. Kubelbeck, Rev. William J., S.T.B., J.C.D., The Sacred Pentitentiaria and Its Relations to Faculties of Ordinaries and Priests, 129 pp., 1918.
6. Petrovits, Rev. Joseph J.C., S.T.D., J.C.D., The New Church Law On Matrimony, X-461 pp., 1919.
7. Hickey, Rev. John J., S.T.B., J.C.D., Irregularities and Simple Impediments in the New Code of Canon Law, 100 pp., 120.
8. Klekotka, Rev. Peter J., S.T.B., J.C.D., Diocesan Consultors, 179 pp., 1920.
9. Wanenmacher, Rev. Francis, J.C.D., The Evidence in Ecclesiastical Procedure Affecting the Marriage Bond, 1920 (Printed 1935).
10. Golden, Rev. Henry Francis, J.C.D., Parochial Benefices in the New Code, IV-119 pp., 1921 (Printed 1925).
11. Koudelka, Rev. Charles J., J.C.D., Pastors, Their Rights and Duties According to the New Code of Canon Law, 211 pp., 1921.
12. Melo, Rev. Antonius, O.F.M., J.C.D., De Exemptione Regularium, X-188 pp., 1921.
13. Schaaf, Rev. Valentine Theodore, O.F.M., S.T.B., J.C.D., The Cloister, X-180 pp., 1921.
14. Burke, Rev. Thomas Joseph, S.T.D., J.C.D., Competence in Ecclesiastical Tribunals, IV-117 pp., 1922.
15. Leech, Rev. George Leo, J.C.D., A Comparative Study of the Constitution, "Apostolicae Sedis" and the "Codex Juris Canonici," 179 pp., 1922.
16. Motry, Rev. Hubert Louis, S.T.D., J.C.D., Diocesan Faculties According to the Code of Canon Law, II-167 pp., 1922.
17. Murphy, Rev. George Lawrence, J.C.D., Delinquencies and Penalties in the Administration and Reception of the Sacraments, IV-121 pp., 1923.
18. O'Reilly, Rev. John Anthony, S.T.B., J.C.D., Ecclesiastical Sepulture in the New Code of Canon Law, II-129 pp., 1923.

19. Michalicka, Rev. Wenceslas Cyrill, O.S.B., J.C.D., Judicial Procedure in Dismissal of Clerical Exempt Religious, 107 pp., 1923.
20. Dargin, Rev. Edward Vincent, S.T.B., J.C.D., Reserved Cases According to the Code of Canon Law, IV-103, pp., 1924.
21. Godfrey, Rev. John A., S.T.B., J.C.D., The Right of Patronage According to the Code of Canon Law, 153 pp., 1924.
22. Hagedorn, Rev. Francis Edward, J.C.D., General Legislation on Indulgences, II-154 pp., 1924.
23. King, Rev. James Ignatius, J.C.D., The Administration of the Sacraments to Dying Non-Catholics, V-141 pp., 1924.
24. Winslow, Rev. Francis Joseph, A.F.M., J.C.D., Vicars and Prefects Apostolic, IV-149 pp., 1924.
25. Correa, Rev. Jose Servelion, S.T.L., J.C.D., La Potestad Legislativa de la Iglesia Catolica, IV-127 pp., 1925.
26. Dugan, Rev. Henry Francis, A.M., J.C.D., The Judiciary Department of the Diocesan Curia, 87 pp., 1925.
27. Keller, Rev. Charles Frederick, S.T.B., J.C.D., Mass Stipends, 167 pp., 1925.
28. Paschang, Rev. John Linus, J.C.D., The Sacramentals According to the Code of Canon Law, 129 pp., 1925.
29. Pointek, Rev. Cyrillus, O.F.M., S.T.B., J.C.D., De Indulto Exclaustrationis necnon Saecularizationis, XIII-289 pp., 1925.
30. Kearney, Rev. Richard Joseph, S.T.B., J.C.D., Sponsors at Baptism According to the Code of Canon Law, IV-127 pp., 1925.
31. Bartlett, Rev. Chester Joseph, A.M., LL.B., J.C.D., The Tenure of Parochial Property in the United States of America, V-108 pp., 1926.
32. Kilker, Rev. Adrian Jerome, J.C.D., Extreme Unction, V-425 pp., 1926.
33. McCormick, Rev. Robert Emmett, J.C.D., Confessors of Religious, VIII-266 pp., 1926.
34. Miller, Rev. Newton Thomas, J.C.D., Founded Masses According to the Code of Canon Law, VII-93 pp., 1926.
35. Roelker, Rev. Edward G., S.T.D., J.C.D., Principles of Privilege According to the Code of Canon Law, XI-166 pp., 1926.
36. Bakalarczyk, Rev. Richardus, M.I.C., J.U.D., De Novitiatu, VIII-208 pp., 1927.
37. Pizzuti, Rev. Lawrence, O.F.M., J.U.L., De Parochis Religiosis, 1927. (Not printed).
38. Bliley, Rev. Nicholas Martin, O.S.B., J.C.D., Altars According to the Code of Canon Law, XIX-132 pp., 1927.
39. Brown, Mr. Brendan Francis, A.B. LL.M., J.U.D., The Canonical Juristic Personality with Special Reference to Its Status in the United States of America, V-212 pp., 1927.

40. Cavanaugh, Rev. William Thomas, C.P., J.U.D., The Reservation of the Blessed Sacrament, VIII-101 pp., 1927.
41. Doheny, Rev. William J., C.S.C., A.B., J.U.D., Church Property: Modes of Acquisition, X-118 pp., 1927.
42. Feldhaus, Rev. Aloysius H., C.PP.S., J.C.D., Oratories, IX-141 pp., 1927.
43. Kelly, Rev. James Patrick, A.B., J.C.D., The Jurisdiction of the Simple Confessor, X-208 pp., 1927.
44. Neuberger, Rev. Nicholas J., J.C.D., Canon 6 or the Relation of the Codex Juris Canonici to the Preceding Legislation, V-95 pp., 1927.
45. O'Keefe, Rev. Gerald Michael, J.C.D., Matrimonial Dispensations, Powers of Bishops, Priests and Confessors, VIII-232 pp., 1927.
46. Quigley, Rev. Joseph A.M., A.B., J.C.B., Condemned Societies, 139 pp., 1927.
47. Zaplotnik, Rev. Johannes Leo, J.C.D., De Vicariis Foraneis, X-142 pp., 1927.
48. Duskie, Rev. John Aloysius, A.B., J.C.D., The Canonical Status of the Orientals in the United States, VIII-196 pp., 1928.
49. Hyland, Rev. Francis Edward, J.C.D., Excommunication, Its Nature, Historical Development and Effects, VIII-181 pp., 1928.
50. Reinmann, Rev. Gerald Joseph, O.M.C., J.C.D., The Third Order Secular of Saint Francis, 201 pp., 1928.
51. Schenk, Rev. Francis J., J.C.D., The Matrimonial Impediments of Mixed Religion and Disparity of Cult, XVI-318 pp., 1929.
52. Coady, Rev. John Joseph, S.T.D., J.U.D., A.M., The Appointment of Pastors, VIII-150 pp., 1929.
53. Kay, Rev. Thomas Henry, J.C.D., Competence in Matrimonial Procedure, VIII-164 pp., 1929.
54. Turner, Rev. Sidney Joseph, C.P., J.U.D., The Vow of Poverty, XLIX-217 pp., 1929.
55. Kearney, Rev. Raymond, A., A.B., S.T.D., J.C.D., The Principles, of Delegation, VII-149 pp., 1929.
56. Conran, Rev. Edward James, A.B., J.C.D., The Interdict, V-163 pp., 1930.
57. O'Neil, Rev. William H., J.C.D., Papal Rescripts of Favor, VII-218 pp., 1930.
58. Bastnagel, Rev. Clement Vincent, J.U.D., The Appointment of Parochial Adjutants and Assistants, XV-257 pp., 1930.
59. Ferry, Rev. William A., A.B., J.C.D., Stole Fees, V-135 pp., 1930.
60. Costello, Rev. John Michael, A.B., J.C.D., Domicile and Quasi-domicile, VII-201 pp., 1930.
61. Kremer, Rev. Michael Nicholas, A.B., S.T.B., J.C.D., Church Support in the United States, VI-1930.

62. Angulo, Rev. Luis, C.M., J.C.D., Legislation de la Iglesia sobre la intencion en la application de la Santa Misa, VII-104 pp., 1931.
63. Frey, Rev. Wolfgang Norbert, O.S.B., A.B., J.C.D., The Act of Religious Profession, VIII-174 pp., 1931.
64. Roberts, Rev. James Brendan, A.B., J.C.D., The Banns of Marriage, XIV-140 pp., 1931.
65. Ryder, Rev. Raymond Aloysius, A.B., J.C.D., Simony, IX-151 pp., 1931.
66. Campagna, Rev. Angelo, Ph.D., J.U.D., Il Vicario Generale del Vescovo, VII-205 pp., 1931.
67. Cox, Rev. Joseph Godfrey, A.B., J.C.D., The Administration ot Seminaries, VI-124 pp., 1931.
68. Gregory, Rev. Donald J., J.U.D., The Pauline Privilege, XV-165 pp., 1931.
69. Donohue, Rev. John F., J.C.D., The Impediment of Crime, VII-110 pp., 1931.
70. Dooley, Rev. Eugene A., O.M.I., J.C.D., Church Law On Sacred Relics, IX-143 pp., 1931.
71. Orth, Rev. Raymond Clement, O.M.C., J.C.D., The Approbation of Religious Institutes, 171 pp., 1931.
72. Pernicone, Rev. Joseph M., A.B., J.C.D., The Ecclesiastical Prohibition of Books, XII-267 pp., 1932.
73. Clinton, Rev. Connell, A.B., J.C.D., The Paschal Precept, IX-108 pp., 1932.
74. Donnelly, Rev. Francis B., A.M., S.T.L., J.C.D., The Diocesan Synod, VIII-125 pp., 1932.
75. Torrente, Rev. Camilo, C.M.F., J.C.D., Las Processiones Sagradas, V-145 pp., 1932.
76. Murphy, Rev. Edwin J., C.PP.S., J.C.D., Suspension Ex Informata Conscientia, XI-122, pp., 1932.
77. Mackenzie, Rev. Eric F., A.M., S.T.L., J.C.D., The Delict of Heresy in its Commission Penalization, Absolution, VII-124 pp., 1932.
78. Lyons Rev. Avitus E., S.T.B., J.C.D., The Collegiate Tribunal of First Instance, XI-147 pp., 1932.
79. Connolly, Rev. Thomas A., J.C.D., Appeals, XI-195 pp., 1932.
80. Sangmeister, Rev. Joseph V., A.B., J.C.D., Force and Fear as Precluding Matrimonial Consent, V-211 pp., 1932.
81. Jaeger, Rev. Leo A., A.B., J.C.D., The Administration of Vacant and Quasi-vacant Episcopal Sees in the United States, IX-229 pp., 1932.
82. Rimlinger, Rev. Herbert T., J.C.D., Error Invalidating Matrimonial Consent, VII-79 pp., 1932.
83. Barrett, Rev. John D.M., S.S., J.C.D., A Comparative Study of the Third Plenary Council of Baltimore and the Code, IX-221 pp., 1932.

84. Carberry, Rev. John J., Ph.D., S.T.D., J.C.D., The Juridical Form of Marriage, X-177 pp., 1934.
85. Dolan, Rev. John L., A.B., J.C.D., The Defensor Vinculi, XII-157 pp., 1934.
86. Hannan, Rev. Jerome D., A.M., S.T.D., LL.B., J.C.D., The Canon Law of Wills, IX-517 pp., 1934.
87. Lemieux, Rev. Delisle A., A.M., J.C.D., The Sentence in Ecclesiastical Procedure, IX-131 pp., 1934.
88. O'Rourke, Rev. James J., A.B., J.C.D., Parish Registers, VII-109 pp., 1934.
89. Timlin, Rev. Bartholomew, O.F.M., A.M., J.C.D., Conditional Matrimonial Consent, X-381 pp., 1934.
90. Wahl, Rev. Francis X., A.B., J.C.D., The Matrimonial Impediments of Consanguinity and Affinity, VI-125 pp., 1934.
91. White, Rev. Robert J., A.B., LL.B., S.T.B., J.C.D., Canonical Ante-Nuptial Promises and the Civil Law, VI-152 pp., 1934.
92. Herrera, Rev. Antonio Parra, O.C.D., J.C.D., Legislation Ecclesiastica sobra el Ayuno y la Abstinencia, XI-191 pp., 1935.
93. Kennedy, Rev. Edwin J., J.C.D., The Special Matrimonial Process in Cases of Evident Nullity, X-165 pp., 1935.
94. Manning, Rev. John J., A.B., J.C.D., Presumption of Law in Matrimonial Procedure, XI-111 pp., 1935.
95. Moeder, Rev. John M., J.C.D., The Proper Bishop for Ordination and Dismissorial Letters, VII-135 pp., 1935.
96. O'Mara, Rev. William A., A.B., J.C.D., Canonical Causes For Matrimonial Dispensations, IX-155 pp., 1935.
97. Reilly, Rev. Peter, J.C.D., Residence of Pastors, IX-81 pp., 1935.
98. Smith, Rev. Mariner T., O.P., S.T.L., J.C.D., The Penal Law For Religious, VII-169 pp., 1935.
99. Whalen, Rev. Donald W., A.M., J.C.D., The Value of Testimonial Evidence in Matrimonial Procedure, XIII-297 pp., 1935.
100. Cleary, Rev. Joseph F., J.C.D., Canonical Limitations on the Alienation of Church Property, VIII-141 pp., 1936.
101. Glynn, Rev. John C., J.C.D., The Promoter of Justice, XX-337 pp., 1936.
102. Brennan, Rev. James H., S.S., A.M., S.T.B., J.C.D., The Simple Convalidation of Marriage, VI-135 pp, 1937.
103. Brunini, Rev. Joseph Bernard, J.C.D., The Clerical Obligations of Canons, 139 and 142, X-121 pp., 1937.
104. Connor, Rev. Maurice, A.B., J.C.D., The Administrative Removal of Pastors, VIII-159 pp., 1937.
105. Guilfoyle, Rev. Merlin Joseph, J.C.D., Custom, XI-144 pp., 1937.
106. Hughes, Rev. James Austin, A.B., A.M., J.C.D., Witnesses in Criminal Trials of Clerics, IX-140 pp., 1937.

107. Jansen, Rev. Raymond J., A.B., S.T.L., J.C.D., Canonical Provisions for Catechetical Instruction, VII-153 pp., 1937.

108. Kealy, Rev. John James, A.B., J.C.D,, The Introductory Libellus in Church Court Procedure, XI-121 pp., 1937.

109. McManus, Rev. James Edward, C.SS.R., J.C.D., The Administration of Temporal Goods in Religious Institutes, XVI-196 pp., 1937.

110. Moriarity, Rev. Eugene James, J.C.D., Oaths in Ecclesiastical Courts, X-115 pp., 1937.

111. Rainer, Rev. Eligius George, C.SS.R., J.C.D., Suspension of Clerics, XVII-249 pp., 1937.

112. Reilly, Rev. Thomas F., C.SS.R., J.C.D., Visitation of Religious, VI-195 pp., 1938.

113. Moriarty, Rev. Francis E., C.SS.R., J.C.D., The Extraordinary Absolution from Censures, XV-334 pp., 1938.

114. Connolly, Rev. Nicholas P., J.C.D., The Canonical Erection of Parishes, X-132 pp., 1938.

115. Donovan, Rev. James Joseph, J.C.D., The Pastor's Obligation in Prenuptial Investigation, XII-322 pp., 1938.

116. Harrigan, Rev. Robert J., M.A., S.T.B., J.C.D., The Radical Sanation of Invalid Marriages, VIII-208 pp., 1938.

117. Boffa, Rev. Conrad Humbert, J.C.D., Canonical Provisions for Catholic Schools, X-211 pp., 1939.

118. Parsons, Rev. Anscar John, O.M. Cap., J.C.D., Canonical Elections, XII-236 pp., 1939.

119. Reilly, Rev. Edward Michael, A.B., J.C.D., The General Norms of Dispensation, X-156 pp., 1939.

120. Ryan, Rev. Gerald Aloysius, A.B., J.C.D., Principles of Episcopal Jurisdiction, XII-172 pp., 1939.

121. Burton, Rev. Francis James, C.S.C., A.B., J.C.D., A Commentary on Canon 1125, X-222 pp., 1940.

122. Miaskiewicz, Rev. Francis Sigismund, J.C.D., Supplied Jurisdiction according to Canon 209, XII-340 pp., 1940.

123. Rice, Rev. Patrick William, A.B., J.C.D., Proof of Death in Prenuptial Investigation, VIII-156 pp., 1940.

124. Anglin, Rev. Thomas Francis. M.S., J.C.L., The Eucharistic Fast.

125. Coleman, Rev. John Jerome, J.C.L., The Minister of Confirmation.

126. Downs, Rev. John Emmanuel, A.B., J.C.L., The Concept of Clerical Immunity.

127. Esswein, Rev. Anthony Albert, J.C.L., Extrajudicial Penal Powers of Ecclesiastical Superiors.

128. Farrell, Rev. Benjamin Francis, M.A., S.T.L., J.C.L., The Rights and Duties of the Local Ordinary Regarding Congregations of Women Religious of Pontifical Approval.

129. Feeney, Rev. Thomas John, A.B., S.T.L., J.C.L., Restitutio in Integrum.
130. Findlay, Rev. Stephen William, O.S.B., A.B., J.C.L., Canonical Norms Governing the Deposition and Degradation of Clerics.
131. Goodwine, Rev. John, A.B., S.T.L., J.C.L., The Right of the Church to Acquire Property.
132. Heston, Rev. Edward Louis, C.S.C., Ph.D., S.T.D., J.C.L., The Alienation of Church Property in the United States .
133. Hogan, Rev. James John, S.T.L., J.C.L.,, Judicial Advocates and Procurators.
134. Kealy, Rev. Thomas M., A.B., Litt. B., J.C.L., Dowry of Women Religious.
135. Keene, Rev. Michael James, O.S.B., J.C.L., Religious Ordinaries and Canon 198.
136. Kerin, Rev. Charles A., S.S., M.A., S.T.B., J.C.L., The Privation of Christian Burial.
137. Louis, Rev. William Francis, M.A., J.C.L., Diocesan Archives.
138. McDevitt, Rev. Gilbert Joseph, A.B., J.C.L., Legitimacy and Legitimation.
139. McDonough, Rev. Thomas Joseph, A.B., J.C.L., Apostolic Administrators.
140. Meier, Rev. Carl Anthony, A.B., J.C.L., Penal Administrative Procedure Against Negligent Pastors.
141. Schmidt, Rev. John Rogg, A.B., J.C.L., The Principles of Authentic Interpretation in Canon 17 of the Code of Canon Law.
142. Slafkosky, Rev. Andrew Leonard, A.B., J.C.L., The Canonical Episcopal Visitation of the Diocese.
143. Swoboda, Rev. Innocent Robert, O.F.M., J.C.L., Ignorance in Relation to the Imputability of Delicts.
144. Dubé, Rev. Arthur Joseph, A.B., J.C.L., The General Principles for the Reckoning of Time in Canon Law.
145. McBride, Rev. James T., A.B., J.C.L., Incardination and Excardination of Seculars.

www.ingramcontent.com/pod-product-compliance
Lightning Source LLC
LaVergne TN
LVHW050230080826
844660LV00012B/509

* 9 7 8 0 8 1 3 2 2 3 1 5 5 *